AAT

Qualifications and Credit Framework (QCF)

AQ2013
LEVEL 4 DIPLOMA IN ACCOUNTING

(QCF)

QUESTION BANK

Cash Management

2014 Edition

For assessments from September 2014

Second edition June 2014
ISBN 9781 4727 0940 0

Previous edition
ISBN 9781 4727 0356 9

British Library Cataloguing-in-Publication Data
A catalogue record for this book is available from the British Library

Published by
BPP Learning Media Ltd
BPP House
Aldine Place
London W12 8AA

www.bpp.com/learningmedia

Printed in the United Kingdom by Martins of Berwick
Sea View Works
Spittal
Berwick-Upon-Tweed
TD15 1RS

Your learning materials, published by BPP Learning Media Ltd, are printed on paper obtained from traceable sustainable sources.

We are grateful to the AAT for permission to reproduce the AAT sample assessment(s). The answers to the AAT sample assessment(s) have been published by the AAT. All other answers have been prepared by BPP Learning Media Ltd.

CONTENTS

Introduction   v

Question and Answer bank

INTRODUCTION

This is BPP Learning Media's AAT Question Bank for Cash Management It is part of a suite of ground breaking resources produced by BPP Learning Media for the AAT's assessments under the qualification and credit framework.

The Cash Management assessment will be **computer assessed**. As well as being available in the traditional paper format, this **Question Bank is available in an online environment** containing tasks similar to those you will encounter in the AAT's testing environment. BPP Learning Media believe that the best way to practise for an online assessment is in an online environment. However, if you are unable to practise in the online environment you will find that all tasks in the paper Question Bank have been written in a style that is as close as possible to the style that you will be presented with in your online assessment.

This Question Bank has been written in conjunction with the BPP Text, and has been carefully designed to enable students to practise all of the learning outcomes and assessment criteria for the units that make up Cash Management. It is fully up to date as at June 2014 and reflects both the AAT's unit guide and the sample assessment(s) provided by the AAT.

This Question Bank contains these key features:

- Tasks corresponding to each chapter of the Text. Some tasks are designed for learning purposes, others are of assessment standard

- The AAT's sample assessment(s) and answers for Cash Management and further BPP practice assessments

The emphasis in all tasks and assessments is on the practical application of the skills acquired.

Approaching the assessment

When you sit the assessment it is very important that you follow the on screen instructions. This means you need to carefully read the instructions, both on the introduction screens and during specific tasks.

When you access the assessment you should be presented with an introductory screen with information similar to that shown below (taken from the introductory screen from one of the AAT's AQ2013 Sample Assessments for Cash Management).

We have provided the following assessment to help you familiarise yourself with AAT's e-assessment environment. It is designed to demonstrate as many as possible of the question types you may find in a live assessment. It is not designed to be used on its own to determine whether you are ready for a live assessment.

Each task is independent. You will not need to refer to your answers to previous tasks.
Read every task carefully to make sure you understand what is required.

Where the date is relevant, it is given in the task data.
Both minus signs and brackets can be used to indicate negative numbers UNLESS task instructions say otherwise.

You must use a full stop to indicate a decimal point.
For example, write 100.57 NOT 100,57 or 100 57

You may use a comma to indicate a number in the thousands, but you don't have to.
For example, 10000 and 10,000 are both OK.

Other indicators are not compatible with the computer-marked system.

Complete all 10 tasks.

The actual instructions will vary depending on the subject you are studying for. It is very important you read the instructions on the introductory screen and apply them in the assessment. You don't want to lose marks when you know the correct answer just because you have not entered it in the right format.

In general, the rules set out in the AAT Sample Assessments for the subject you are studying for will apply in the real assessment, but you should again read the information on this screen in the real assessment carefully just to make sure. This screen may also confirm the VAT rate used if applicable.

A full stop is needed to indicate a decimal point. We would recommend using minus signs to indicate negative numbers and leaving out the comma signs to indicate thousands, as this results in a lower number of key strokes and less margin for error when working under time pressure. Having said that, you can use whatever is easiest for you as long as you operate within the rules set out for your particular assessment.

You have to show competence throughout the assessment and you should therefore complete all of the tasks. Don't leave questions unanswered.

In some assessments written or complex tasks may be human marked. In this case you are given a blank space or table to enter your answer into. You are told in the practice assessments which tasks these are (note: there may be none if all answers are marked by the computer).

If these involve calculations, it is a good idea to decide in advance how you are going to lay out your answers to such tasks by practising answering them on a word document, and certainly you should try all such tasks in this question bank and in the AAT's environment using the sample assessments.

When asked to fill in tables, or gaps, never leave any blank even if you are unsure of the answer. Fill in your best estimate.

Note that for some assessments where there is a lot of scenario information or tables of data provided (eg tax tables), you may need to access these via 'pop-ups'. Instructions will be provided on how you can bring up the necessary data during the assessment.

Finally, take note of any task specific instructions once you are in the assessment. For example you may be asked to enter a date in a certain format or to enter a number to a certain number of decimal places.

Remember you can practise the BPP questions in this question bank in an online environment on our dedicated AAT Online page. On the same page is a link to the current AAT Practice Assessments as well.

If you have any comments about this book, please email ianblackmore@bpp.com or write to Ian Blackmore, Range Manager, BPP Learning Media Ltd, BPP House, Aldine Place, London W12 8AA.

Question bank

Chapter 1 – Cash flow and profit

Task 1.1

Selecting from the picklists complete the following sentences.

If a business makes a profit this means that [▼]

Picklist:

Its cash inflows are greater than its cash outflow.
Its revenue is greater than its expenses.

Cash flow and profit will [▼] be the same figure for a period.

Picklist:

Normally
Not normally

Task 1.2

Give FIVE reasons why there might be a difference between the profit of a business and its cash balance.

1

2

3

4

5

Task 1.3

Given below is the forecast statement of profit or loss for a business for the three months ending 31 December together with forecast statements of financial position at that date and also at the previous 30 September.

Forecast Statement of profit or loss for the three months ending 31 December

	£'000
Revenue	860
Cost of sales	(600)
Gross profit	260
Depreciation	(20)
Overheads	(100)
Profit from operations	140

Forecast statements of financial position

	31 December £'000	31 December £'000	30 September £'000	30 September £'000
Non-current assets		1,050		760
Current assets:				
Inventory	100		100	
Receivables	85		45	
Cash	10		10	
	195		155	
Payables	100		75	
Accruals of overheads	45		40	
	145		115	
Net current assets		50		40
		1,100		800
Equity share capital		600		600
Retained earnings		500		200
		1,100		800

Calculate the actual cash receipts and cash payments for the quarter to 31 December.

	£'000
Sales receipts	
Purchase payments	
Overhead payments	

Task 1.4

The carrying amount of non-current assets on 1 January was £125,000 and the statement of financial position at 31 December shows non-current assets of £152,000. During the year £12,500 depreciation was charged. There were no non-current asset disposals.

What was the cash paid to acquire non-current assets in the year ended 31 December?

£12,500 ☐

£14,500 ☐

£27,000 ☐

£39,500 ☐

Task 1.5

A business decides to sell one of its machines. The machine being sold originally cost £64,400. At the date of disposal, accumulated depreciation on the machine amounts to £38,640. The machine is sold for £23,800.

What was the profit or loss on disposal of the machine?

£1,960 profit ☐

£1,960 loss ☐

£14,840 profit ☐

£14,840 loss ☐

Task 1.6

A business decides to sell one of its buildings which originally cost £105,000 and on which, at the date of disposal, accumulated depreciation amounted to £48,500. The sale generated a profit on disposal of £35,000.

What were the cash proceeds on disposal of the building?

£21,500 ☐

£56,500 ☐

£70,000 ☐

£91,500 ☐

Task 1.7

The following information has been extracted from the Sales Ledger Control Account for the year ended 31 July:

	£
Opening trade receivables	34,500
Closing trade receivables	47,900
Sales revenue per statement of profit or loss	252,000

Sales revenue per statement of profit

Closing trade receivables

Opening trade receivables

34,500

47,900

252,000

Drag and drop the descriptions and figures above to the correct place in the control account then complete the account to determine the cash received from customers during the year:

Sales Ledger Control Account			
	Dr £		Cr £
		Cash received	
	_____		
	_____		_____

Chapter 2 – Forecasting income and expenditure

Task 2.1

Given below are the daily takings in a shop that is open five days a week, Monday to Friday.

	Mon £	Tues £	Wed £	Thurs £	Fri £
Week 1	1,260	1,600	1,630	1,780	1,830
Week 2	1,340	1,750	1,640	1,850	1,980
Week 3	1,550	1,660	1,620	1,870	1,970

Calculate the five-day moving average for the daily takings.

Week	Day	Takings £	Five-day moving average £

Task 2.2

In time series analysis there are a number of elements of a time series.

Match each element of a time series analysis listed on the left with its correct description from the list on the right.

Random variation	Variations in the time series due to the seasonality of the business
Trend	Long-term variations caused by general economic factors
Cyclical variation	Other variations not due to the trend, cyclical or seasonal variations
Seasonal variation	General movement in the time series figure

Task 2.3

A company is trying to estimate its sales volumes for the first three months of next year. This is to be done by calculating a trend using the actual monthly sales volumes for the current year and a 3-point moving average.

(a) **Complete the table below to calculate the monthly sales volume trend and identify any monthly variations.**

	Sales volume Units	Trend Units	Monthly variation (volume less trend) Units
January	20,000		
February	17,400		
March	16,300		
April	22,400		
May	19,800		
June	18,700		
July	24,800		
August	22,200		
September	21,100		
October	27,200		
November	24,600		
December	23,500		

The monthly sales volume trend is [   ] units.

(b) **Using the trend and the monthly variations identified in part (a) complete the table below for forecast sales volume for January, February and March of the next financial year.**

	Forecast trend Units	Variation Units	Forecast sales volume Units
January			
February			
March			

Task 2.4

Trend values for sales of barbecues by Hothouse Ltd over the last three years have been as follows:

Year	1st quarter	2nd quarter	3rd quarter	4th quarter
1	7,494	7,665	7,890	8,123
2	8,295	8,493	8,701	8,887
3	9,090	9,296	9,501	9,705

Average seasonal variations for the four quarters have been:

Quarter 1 + 53
Quarter 2 + 997
Quarter 3 + 1,203
Quarter 4 – 2,253

Use the trend and estimates of seasonal variations to forecast sales in each quarter of next year and the associated revenue if the selling price is expected to be £45 per barbecue.

Average increase in trend value [   ] units

Future trend values

Quarter 1 [   ]

Quarter 2 [   ]

Quarter 3 [   ]

Quarter 4 [   ]

Quarter	Trend forecast	Average seasonal variation	Forecast of actual sales units	Forecast revenue £
1				
2				
3				
4				

BPP LEARNING MEDIA

Task 2.5

A business currently sells its product for £30 but it is anticipated that there will be a price increase of 4% from 1 February. The sales quantities are expected to be as follows:

January	21,000 units
February	22,000 units
March	22,800 units

All sales are on credit and 40% of cash is received in the month following the sale and the remainder two months after the sale.

What are the receipts from sales that are received in March?

	£
January sales	
February sales	
Total March receipts	

Task 2.6

A business has production overheads of £347,000 in December 20X8 but it is anticipated that these will increase by 1.25% per month for the next few months. Overheads are paid the month after they are incurred.

What is the cash outflow for overheads that is paid during the month of March 20X9 (to the nearest whole £)?

£347,000 ☐

£355,729 ☐

£351,338 ☐

£360,176 ☐

Task 2.7

A business makes purchases of a raw material which has a cost of £2.60 per kg in November 20X8. The actual and estimated price index for this material is as follows:

	Price index
November (actual)	166.3
December (estimate)	169.0
January (estimate)	173.4
February (estimate)	177.2

What is the expected price per kg (to the nearest penny) of the raw material in each of the months of December, January and February?

	£
December	
January	
February	

Task 2.8

A company, which is growing, has prepared the following regression equation as a basis for estimating sales (Y) in units for the relevant period (X).

$Y = 27X - 24$

Quarterly seasonal variations affecting sales levels are as follows.

Q1	Q2	Q3	Q4
−25%	−25%	+15%	+35%

Period 12 is in quarter 4. **What is the forecast sales level for period 12?**

Forecast P12 sales [   ] units

Task 2.9

Sales are often considered to be the principal budget factor of an organisation.

Explain the meaning and relevance of the 'principal budget factor'. Assuming that it is sales, explain possible methods of forecasting sales, making appropriate reference to the use of statistical techniques.

Task 2.10

(a) A company uses time series analysis and regression techniques to estimate future sales demand. Using these techniques, it has derived the following trend equation:

$y = 10,000 + 4,200x$

where y is the total sales units; and

x is the time period

It has also derived the following seasonal variation index values for each of the quarters using the multiplicative seasonal variation model:

Quarter	Index value
1	120
2	80
3	95
4	105

What are the total sales units that will be forecast for time period 33, which is the first quarter of year 9?

(b) Time series analysis and regression techniques are based on extrapolations of past performance into the future in order to provide information for planning and decision making.

Discuss the problems of extrapolating past performance into the future.

Chapter 3 – Patterns of cash flows

Task 3.1

Cash receipts and payments take many different forms which may include regular receipts and payments, irregular receipts and payments, capital payments and drawings/dividends.

Complete the table by dragging and dropping the appropriate example to match the correct type of cash receipt or cash payment.

Type of receipt/payment	Example
Regular revenue receipts	
Regular revenue payments	
Exceptional receipts/payments	
Capital payments/receipts	
Drawings/dividends	

The drag and drop choices are:

Income received from HM Revenue and Customs

Income received from the operating activities of the business which are expected to occur frequently

Income received from the operating activities of the business which are not expected to occur frequently

Income that arises from the proceeds of the sale of non-current assets

Payments that arise from the acquisition of non-current assets

Income received from the owner of the business

Payments made to the owner of the business

Payments due to the operating activities of the business that are expected to be incurred frequently

Payments due to the operating activities of the business that are not expected to be incurred frequently

••

Task 3.2

A business makes 30% of its monthly sales for cash with the remainder being sold on credit. On average 40% of the total sales are received in the month following the sale and the remainder in the second month after the sale. Sales figures are estimated to be as follows.

	£
August	240,000
September	265,000
October	280,000
November	250,000
December	220,000

What are the cash receipts from sales that are received in each of the three months from October to December? Round to the nearest whole £.

Cash Sales	October £	November £	December £
Cash Sales			
October			
November			
December			
Credit sales			
August			
September			
September			
October			
October			
November			
Total cash receipts			

Task 3.3

A business purchases all of its goods on credit from suppliers. 20% of purchases are offered a discount of 2% for payment in the month of purchase and the business takes advantage of these discounts. A further 45% of purchases are paid for in the month after the purchase and the remainder are paid for two months after the purchase. Purchases figures are estimated to be as follows.

	£
August	180,000
September	165,000
October	190,000
November	200,000
December	220,000

What are the cash payments made to suppliers in each of the three months from October to December? Round to the nearest whole £.

	October £	November £	December £

Task 3.4

A retail business buys flowers from a wholesaler, adds a mark-up of 50% on cost and then sells them to its customers, in the month of purchase, for cash.

If purchases for the three months from January to March are as follows, what are the monthly cash sales? Round to the nearest whole £.

	January £	February £	March £
Purchases	22,000	24,000	26,000
Cash sales			

The margin that the retailer is making is ☐ %.

Task 3.5

(a) A business makes all of its sales on credit with a 3% settlement discount offered for payment within the month of the sale. 25% of sales take up this settlement discount and 70% of sales are paid in the following month. The remainder are irrecoverable debts.

Sales figures are as follows.

	£
March	650,000
April	600,000
May	580,000
June	550,000

What are the cash receipts from sales that are received in each of the three months from April to June? Round to the nearest whole £.

	April £	May £	June £
Total cash receipts			

BPP
LEARNING MEDIA

(b) The business is considering the effect of increasing the settlement discount to 5%. As a result, with effect from March sales, 30% of customers are expected to take the discount and all remaining customers to pay in the following month, with no irrecoverable debts.

What are the revised cash receipts from sales? Round to the nearest whole £.

	April £	May £	June £
Total cash receipts			

Task 3.6

(a) A company's trade receivables balance at the beginning of the year was £22,000. The statement of profit or loss showed revenue from credit sales of £290,510 during the year . The trade receivables days at the end of the year were 49 days.

Assume that:

- Sales occur evenly throughout the year
- All balances outstanding at the start of the year were received
- All sales are on credit and there were no irrecoverable debts
- No trade discount was given

How much cash did the company receive from its customers during the year?

(b) A company has a balance outstanding on its trade receivables account at the start of the year of £83,000 after allowing for irrecoverable debts. The company forecasts sales revenue for the next year of £492,750. All sales are on credit.

Based on past experience, irrecoverable debts represent 5% of sales revenue. Trade receivable days at the end of the year are expected to be 60 days.

What are the expected cash receipts from customers during the year (to the nearest penny)?

Task 3.7

A company manufactures and sells a single product. The company is preparing its cash budget for next year. The company divides the year into four periods, each of thirteen weeks. Sales and production will occur evenly within each period. Details are as follows:

Sales budget (810,000 units)

The selling price is £30 per unit. All sales will be on credit and payment will be received five weeks after the date of sale. It is expected that 2% of all sales will become irrecoverable debts. The budgeted sales units are:

Period	1	2	3	4
Sales (units)	150,000	200,000	180,000	280,000

The product incurs variable selling costs of £1.60 per unit. These are paid in the period in which they are incurred.

Production budget (860,000 units)

Period	1	2	3	4
Production (units)	210,000	210,000	220,000	220,000

Production cost per unit

	£	Notes
Raw materials	9.50	Purchased on credit. Paid for four weeks after purchase. See below.
Production wages	8.20	Paid one week in arrears. These are variable costs.
Production expenses	7.00	See below.
	24·70	

Raw material inventory

The company wishes to increase inventory to cover six weeks of future production by the end of Period 1 and then to seven weeks by the end of Period 2. Purchases will occur evenly throughout each period.

Production expenses

The production expenses of £7.00 per unit comprise the following:

	£	Notes
Variable production expenses	1.10	Paid in the period incurred.
Fixed production expenses:		
Depreciation	2.70	This is an annual fixed cost that is absorbed on a per unit basis over the budgeted production of 860,000 units.
Other fixed expenses	3.20	Cost per unit based on the annual production of 860,000 units. Fixed expenses are paid in two equal instalments at the beginning of periods 1 and 3.

Long term borrowing

The company has a long term loan. The balance on this loan at the start of the year will be £10m. Interest on this loan is charged at 9% per annum on the amount outstanding at the start of the year. It is to be paid in two equal instalments at the end of period 2 and at the end of period 4. The loan is 'interest only' - there are no capital repayments due.

Opening balances

	£	
Raw materials inventory	710,000	(all purchased at the current price)
Trade receivables	2,430,000	(net of irrecoverable debts)
Bank and cash	76,000	
Trade payables	612,000	
Unpaid wages	130,000	
Loan	10,000,000	

Prepare, showing all cash flows to the nearest £'000, a cash budget for period 1 and period 2. Use brackets or minus signs where appropriate.

	Period 1 £'000	Period 2 £'000
Sales receipts		
Raw material purchases		
Production wages		
Variable production expenses		
Variable selling expenses		
Fixed production expenses		
Interest		
Net cash flow for the period		
Opening cash balance		
Closing cash balance		

Chapter 4 – Preparing cash budgets

Task 4.1

A company pays interest at 13% per annum on its overdraft.

Two of the company's suppliers, X and Y are offering the following terms for immediate cash settlement.

Company	Discount	Normal settlement period
X	3%	3 months
Y	4%	4 months

(a) **Which of the following discounts should be accepted?**

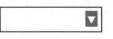

Picklist:

X only
Y only
Both X and Y
Neither X nor Y

The company is also concerned about the increasing level of trade receivables and is considering various options to encourage customers to pay earlier. The company currently offers 30 day payment terms but customers are taking on average 65 days to pay.

One option being considered is to offer an early settlement discount of 2.5% for customers paying within 15 days.

(b) **Calculate, to the nearest 0.1%, the effective annual interest rate to the company of offering this discount if all customers pay within 15 days. You should assume a 365 day year and use compound interest methodology.**

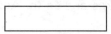

(c) A company has annual sales revenue of £4 million and credit terms are 30 days, although customers on average take 40 days to pay. The company currently has no irrecoverable debts. Accounts receivable are financed by an overdraft at an annual interest rate of 5%.

The company plans to offer an early settlement discount of 2% for payment within 10 days and to extend the maximum credit offered to 60 days. The company expects that these changes will increase annual credit sales by 8%. The gross profit margin on sales is 50% and the change in credit policy will give rise to additional administration costs, equal to 1% of total sales revenue. The discount is expected to be taken by 25% of customers, with the remaining customers taking an average of 50 days to pay. There will be no irrecoverable debts.

Evaluate the impact of the proposed changes in credit policy on profitability

```
┌─────────────────────────────────────────────────────────────────────────────┐
│                                                                               │
│                                                                               │
│                                                                               │
│                                                                               │
│                                                                               │
│                                                                               │
│                                                                               │
│                                                                               │
│                                                                               │
│                                                                               │
│                                                                               │
│                                                                               │
│                                                                               │
└───────────────────────────────────────────────────────────────────────────────┘
```

Task 4.2

A manufacturing company is preparing its cash budget for the three months ending 31 July. The production budget is estimated to be as follows.

	April	May	June	July	August
Production quantity	1,020	1,220	1,320	1,520	1,620

The materials required for the product are 2 kg per unit costing £40 per kg and are purchased in the month prior to production and paid for in the following month. At 1 April there are 550 kgs of raw material in inventory but these are to be reduced by 50 kgs per month for each of the next four months.

(a) **Use the table below to complete the purchases budget in kgs and £s for April to July**

	April Kgs	May Kgs	June Kgs	July Kgs
Materials required for production				
April				
May				
June				
July				
Opening inventory				
Closing inventory				
Purchases in kgs				

	April £	May £	June £	July £
April				
May				
June				
July				

(b) **Calculate the cash payments to suppliers for May to July**

	May £	June £	July £
Cash payments			

Task 4.3

A business manufactures and sells a single product, each unit of which requires 20 minutes of labour. The wage rate is £8.40 per hour. The production budget is anticipated to be:

	April	May	June	July
Sales in units	7,200	7,050	6,450	6,000

The product is produced one month prior to sale and wages are paid in the month of production.

Calculate the cash payments for wages for each of the three months from April to June.

Labour budget – hours	April Hours	May Hours	June Hours
April			
May			
June			
Labour budget – £	April £	May £	June £
April			
May			
June			

Task 4.4

A business is about to prepare a cash budget for the quarter ending 30 September. The recent actual and estimated sales figures are as follows.

	£
April (actual)	420,000
May (actual)	400,000
June (estimate)	480,000
July (estimate)	500,000
August (estimate)	520,000
September (estimate)	510,000

All sales are on credit and the payment pattern is as follows.
20% pay in the month of sale after taking a 4% settlement discount.
40% pay in the month following the sale.
25% pay two months after the month of sale.
12% pay three months after the month of sale.
There are expected to be 3% irrecoverable debts.

(a) **Complete the table below to show the cash receipts from customers**.

		July £	August £	September £
April sales				
May sales				
June sales				
July sales				
August sales				
September sales				
Total receipts				

The purchases of the business are all on credit and it is estimated that the following purchases will be made.

	£
May	250,000
June	240,000
July	280,000
August	300,000
September	310,000

40% of purchases are paid for in the month after the purchase has been made and the remainder are paid for two months after the month of purchase.

(b) **Complete the table below to show the cash payments to suppliers.**

		July £	August £	September £
May purchases				
June purchases				
July purchases				
August purchases				
Total payments				

General overheads are anticipated to be a monthly £50,000 for June and July increasing to £55,000 thereafter. 75% of the general overheads are paid in the month in which they are incurred and the remainder in the following month. The general overheads figure includes a depreciation charge of £6,000 each month.

(c) **Complete the table below to show the cash payments for general overheads.**

		July £	August £	September £
June overheads				
July overheads				
August overheads				
September overheads				
Total overhead payments				

Additional information

- Wages are expected to be £60,000 each month and are paid in the month in which they are incurred.

- Selling expenses are expected to be 10% of the monthly sales value and are paid for in the month following the sale.

- The business has planned to purchase new equipment for £42,000 in August and in the same month to dispose of old equipment with estimated sales proceeds of £7,500.

- Overdraft interest is charged at 1% per month based on the overdraft balance at the start of the month. At 1 July it is anticipated that the business will have an overdraft of £82,000.

(d) **Referring to your answers in parts (a), (b) and (c) and the additional information above, prepare a monthly cash budget for the three months ending September.** Cash inflows should be entered as positive figures and cash outflows as negative figures. Zeros must be entered where appropriate to achieve full marks.

	July £	August £	September £
Receipts			
Receipts from credit sales			
Proceeds from sale of equipment			
Total receipts			
Payments			
Payments to suppliers			
Wages			
Overheads			
Selling expenses			
Equipment			
Overdraft interest			
Total payments			
Net cash flow			
Opening balance			
Closing balance			

Task 4.5

A manufacturing business is to prepare its cash budget for the three months ending 31 December. The business manufactures a single product which requires 3 kg of raw material per unit and 3 hours of labour per unit. Production is in the month of sale. The raw material cost is anticipated to be £9 per kg and the labour force is paid at a rate of £7.20 per hour. Each unit of the product sells for £75.

The forecast sales in units are as follows:

	August	September	October	November	December
Forecast sales – units	5,000	5,100	5,400	5,800	6,000

Sales are on credit with 40% of customers paying the month after sale and the remainder two months after the sale.

(a) **Complete the table below to calculate the timing of receipts from credit customers to be included in the cash budget.**

		October £	November £	December £
August sales				
September sales				
October sales				
November sales				
Total cash receipts				

The raw materials required for production are purchased in the month prior to production and 60% are paid for in the following month and the remainder two months after purchase. The anticipated inventory of raw materials is 3,000 kgs until the end of September and the planned inventory levels at the end of each month thereafter are as follows:

October   3,200 kgs
November   3,500 kgs
December   4,000 kgs

The production budget is as follows:	Aug Units	Sept Units	Oct Units	Nov Units	Dec Units
Production	5,000	5,100	5,500	5,900	6,100

(b) **Complete the following table to give the purchases budget for August to November in both kgs and £.**

	Aug kg	Sept kg	Oct kg	Nov kg
Kgs required for production				
Opening inventory				
Closing inventory				
Purchases in kgs				
	£	£	£	£
Purchases in £				

(c) **Using the information from part (b) and above complete the following table to calculate the payments to suppliers for October to December.**

		Oct £	Nov £	Dec £
August purchases				
September purchases				
October purchases				
November purchases				
Total cash payments				

Wages are paid in the month in which they are incurred.

(d) **Complete the table below to show the labour budget for October to December in hours and in £.**

	Oct Hours	Nov Hours	Dec Hours
Production times hours per unit			
	£	£	£
Production hours times wage rate			

Additional information

- Production overheads are expected to be £60,000 each month and are paid for in the month in which they are incurred. This figure includes depreciation of £10,000 per month for machinery.

- General overheads are anticipated to be £72,000 each month in October and November increasing to £80,000 in December and are paid in the month in which they are incurred. The figure for general overheads includes £12,000 of depreciation each month.

- The cash balance at 1 October is expected to be £40,000 in credit.

(e) **Referring to your answers in parts (a) to (d) and the additional information above, prepare a monthly cash budget for the three months ending December. Cash inflows should be entered as positive figures and cash outflows as negative figures. Zeroes must be entered where appropriate to achieve full marks.**

	October £	November £	December £
Receipts			
From credit customers			
Payments			
To credit suppliers			
Wages			
Production overheads			
General overheads			
Total payments			
Net cash flow			
Opening bank balance			
Closing bank balance			

Task 4.6

A business currently pays its suppliers with the following pattern:

60% one month after the date of purchase
40% two months after the date of purchase

On 30% of these purchases a 3% discount is offered for payment during the month of purchase but in the past the business has not taken advantage of this. If it did take advantage then 30% of purchases would be paid for in the month of purchase, 40% in the month following purchase and 30% two months after the date of purchase.

Purchases are estimated to be as follows:

	£
August	520,000
September	550,000
October	560,000
November	580,000
December	600,000

(a) **Using the table below calculate the payments to suppliers in October, November and December in accordance with the current situation where no settlement discounts are taken.**

	October £	November £	December £
August purchases			
September purchases			
October purchases			
November purchases			
Total cash payments			

(b) **Using the table below calculate the payments made to suppliers in October, November and December in accordance with the new settlement discount scheme described above on the assumption that the scheme begins in October.**

	October £	November £	December £
August purchases			
September purchases			
October purchases			
November purchases			
December purchases			
Total cash payments			

Task 4.7

(a) At 31 March a business had receivables of £260,000. Planned sales for the following three months in units are:

April	140,000 units
May	150,000 units
June	155,000 units

All sales are made on credit. On average 40% of receivables pay during the month after the sale and the remainder pay two months after the date of sale.

The receivables at 31 March can be assumed to pay as follows:

	£
In April	140,000
In May	120,000
	260,000

Sales are made at a price of £1.00 per unit.

However, in the light of current economic circumstances it is being anticipated that the sales price will have to be reduced to £0.90 per unit.

Use the table below to calculate the effect of the changes in the forecast amounts for April, May and June.

	April £	May £	June £
Original value of forecast sales			
Original timing of receipts			
Revised value of forecast sales			
Revised timing of receipts			
Increase/(decrease) in sales receipts			

(b) An extract from the original cash budget is set out below.

	April £	May £	June £
Net cash flow	(12,000)	40,000	44,000
Opening bank balance	(20,000)	(32,000)	8,000
Closing bank balance	(32,000)	8,000	52,000

Using your calculation of the revised receipts in (a) above, complete the table to show the impact of the change in the forecast amounts on the budgeted bank balances.

	April £	May £	June £
Original net cash flow	(12,000)	40,000	44,000
Increase/(decrease) in sales receipts per (a)			
Revised net cash flow			
Opening bank balance			
Closing bank balance			

Task 4.8

A company is considering its sales budget for the next year. It is expected that sales will be 20,000 units at a selling price of £3.00 per unit. Variable costs are expected to be £1.65 per unit, while fixed costs are expected to be £20,000 per year.

The company wants to know how much flexibility it has to offer discounts on the sales price.

(a) Explain how sensitivity analysis can help the company to decide on its plans.

(b) **Calculate the sensitivity of the company's profits to a change in each of the following variables. Express your answer as a % to the nearest 2 decimal places:**

(i)   Sales volume

(ii)   Sales price

(iii) Variable costs

Task 4.9

A company is preparing its cash budget for the next quarter. In October the quarterly sales tax (VAT) payment relating to June, July and August, is to be paid. Standard rated sales for the three months were £2,125,000 and standard rated purchases were £1,975,000. (Standard rate VAT is 20%.).

(a) **How much VAT will be due to HM Revenue and Customs in October?**

(b) **When is VAT normally due?**

One month and 9 days after the end of the relevant VAT period

One month and 1 day after the end of the relevant VAT period

One month and 7 days after the end of the relevant VAT period

Chapter 5 – Monitoring cash flows

Task 5.1

Given below is the cash budget for the month of June for a business together with the actual cash flows for the month of June.

Cash budget June

	Budget £	Actual £
Receipts:		
Cash sales receipts	101,000	94,000
Credit sales receipts	487,000	475,000
Total receipts	588,000	569,000
Payments:		
Credit suppliers	(303,000)	(294,000)
Wages	(155,000)	(162,000)
Variable overheads	(98,600)	(99,400)
Fixed overheads	(40,000)	(40,000)
Capital expenditure	–	(45,000)
Total payments	(596,600)	(640,400)
Net cash flow for the month	(8,600)	(71,400)
Bank b/f	20,300	20,300
Bank c/f	11,700	(51,100)

Complete the table below to compare the actual cash flows to the budgeted cash flows and identify any variances indicating whether they are favourable or adverse variances.

	Budget £	Actual £	Variance £	Adv/Fav £
Receipts:				
Cash sales receipts				
Credit sales receipts				
Total receipts				
Payments:				
Credit suppliers				
Wages				
Variable overheads				
Fixed overheads				
Capital expenditure				
Total payments				
Net cash flow				
Balance b/f				
Balance c/f				

Task 5.2

Given below is the cash budget and actual cash flows for a business for the month of July.

	Budget £	Actual £
Receipts:		
Cash sales	264,000	277,000
Receipts from credit customers	888,000	863,000
Proceeds from sale of non-current assets	–	22,000
Total receipts	1,152,000	1,162,000
Payments:		
Payments to credit suppliers	742,000	777,000
Wages	197,000	197,000
Variable overheads	51,300	58,700
Fixed overheads	66,000	68,000
Purchase of non-current assets	–	46,000
Dividend payment	50,000	50,000
Total payments	1,106,300	1,196,700
Net cash flow	45,700	(34,700)
Opening cash balance	16,200	16,200
Closing cash balance	61,900	(18,500)

(a) **Reconcile the budgeted cash balance at 31 July to the actual cash balance at that date using the table below. Select the appropriate description for each entry. Clearly indicate whether figures are to be added or deducted in the reconciliation by entering minus signs where appropriate.**

	£
Budgeted closing bank balance	
Surplus/shortfall in cash sales	
Surplus/shortfall in credit sales receipts	
Increase/decrease in proceeds from sales from non-current assets	
Increase/decrease/no change in payments to credit suppliers	
Increase/decrease in wages	
Increase/decrease in variable overheads	
Increase/decrease in fixed overheads	
Increase/decrease in purchase of non-current assets	
Increase/decrease/no change in dividend payments	
Actual closing bank balance	

(b) **What actions could have been taken to avoid the use of overdraft finance by the end of the month?**

Delay capital expenditure ☐

Chase customers to pay sooner ☐

Delay payments to suppliers ☐

Marketing campaign to increase sales ☐

Task 5.3

(a) **A business is in the process of comparing its budgeted and actual cash flows for February. Complete the table below to identify any variances indicating whether they are favourable (+) or adverse (-) variances.**

	Budget February £	Actual February £	Variance £
Cash receipts			
Receipts from sales	148,800	145,600	
Deposit account interest	100	100	
Total cash receipts	**148,900**	**145,700**	
Cash payments			
Payments to suppliers	–41,600	–56,000	
Salaries	–43,000	–45,150	
Administration overheads	–30,000	–30,000	
Capital expenditure	–20,000	–6,000	
Total payments	**–134,600**	**–137,150**	
Net cash flow	**14,300**	**8,550**	
Opening cash balance	–25,900	–25,900	
Closing cash balance	**–11,600**	**–17,350**	

(b) **Reconcile the budgeted cash balance at end February to the actual cash balance at that date using the table below. Select the appropriate description for each entry. Clearly indicate whether figures are to be added or deducted in the reconciliation by entering minus signs where appropriate.**

	£
Budgeted closing bank balance	
Surplus/shortfall in sales receipts	
Surplus/shortfall/no change in deposit account interest	
Increase/decrease in payments to credit suppliers	
Increase/decrease in salaries	
Increase/decrease/no change in administration overheads	
Increase/decrease in capital expenditure	
Actual closing bank balance	

(c) **From the picklist below, choose the appropriate explanations for the variances identified.**

Sales receipts	▼

Payments to suppliers	▼

Salaries	▼

Capital expenditure	▼

Picklist:

Increase product selling price
Cut back on overtime working
Negotiated credit with supplier of equipment, provided initial deposit paid in month of purchase
Issued less share capital
Loss of customers
Used up material from inventory
Bonus paid to staff
Increase in suppliers prices

Task 5.4

Variances between actual cash flows and budgeted cash flows can be due to a variety of reasons. There are also a number of courses of action which are available to minimise the effect of adverse variances and to capitalise on the benefit of favourable variances.

Match each variance listed on the left with a possible course of action from the list on the right.

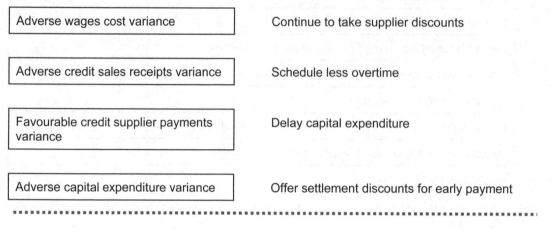

| Adverse wages cost variance | Continue to take supplier discounts |

| Adverse credit sales receipts variance | Schedule less overtime |

| Favourable credit supplier payments variance | Delay capital expenditure |

| Adverse capital expenditure variance | Offer settlement discounts for early payment |

Task 5.5

(a) Actual payments for overheads in a period were £27,500 and there was an adverse overhead expenditure variance of £1,200.

   What was the budgeted figure for overheads?

    £ [   ]

(b) In April a business actually spent £18,000 on the purchase of a non-current asset, giving rise to a favourable variance of £2,300.

   How much did the business budget for the cost of the non-current asset?

   £ [   ]

Task 5.6

You are provided with the following information about cash flow relating to a new product in the first month of its launch.

	Budget	Actual
Sales (units)	72,000	64,000
Selling price	£10 per unit	£8.40 per unit
Cash received from sales	£720,000	£430,080

(a) **Calculate the following variances, indicating if each is adverse (Adv) or favourable (Fav).**

	Budget	Actual	Variance	Adv/Fav
Sales (units)	72,000	64,000		
Selling price (£ per unit)	£10 per unit	£8.40 per unit		
Cash received from sales (£)	£720,000	£430,080		

(b) **Comment briefly on the possible causes of a variance.**

(c) **Explain the major benefit of analysing variances.**

(d) **Briefly explain three factors that you would consider before deciding to investigate a variance.**

Task 5.7

'Variance analysis presents results after the actual events have taken place and therefore it is of little use to management for planning and control purposes, particularly in a modern manufacturing environment'.

Discuss the above statement.

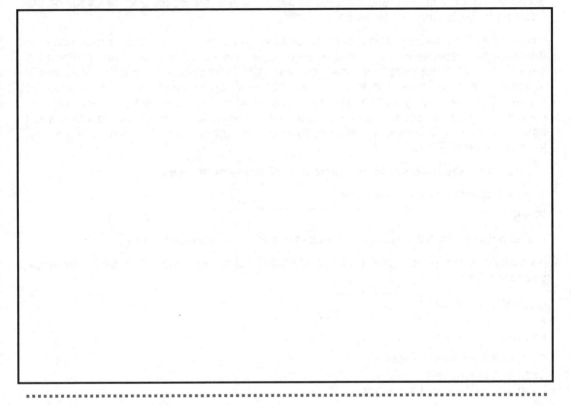

Chapter 6 – Liquidity management

Task 6.1

You work in a small business which installs fire alarms. As the only member of the accounts department, you report directly to the proprietor, Mr Blaze. One day, you find the following long note from Mr Blaze on your table.

'I've been to the bank and asked them to lend me some money. I've always had money in the bank, but because the loan is to acquire some new equipment, the bank wants a full set of financial statements. The manager asked for statements of profit or loss and a statement of cash flows. He then started jabbering on in jargon I didn't understand: something about *cash operating cycle times*, as he said they were relevant. I also said we were a profitable business. Then he said he needed some ideas as to how *liquid* we are. I said we were a solid company, we've been trading for many years. He said I'd better chat to an accountant. Please help!'

Choose from the picklists to complete the following sentences.

The cash operating cycle time is the [▼]

Picklist:

Period between cash being paid for purchases and cash received for sales

Inventory holding period plus trade receivables' collection period less trade payables' payment period

Liquid assets include [▼]

Picklist:

Cash and short-term investments
Cash and fixed assets
Cash, receivables and inventory

Task 6.2

Kitten Ltd buys raw materials on three months' credit, holds them in store for four months and then issues them to production. The production cycle is a couple of days, and then finished goods are held for one month before they are sold. Credit customers are normally allowed two months' credit.

What is Kitten Ltd's cash operating cycle in months?

1 month   [ ]

2 months   [ ]

3 months   [ ]

4 months   [ ]

Task 6.3

During the year ending 30 June a business had a cash operating cycle of 87 days. It had a trade receivables' collection period of 77 days and trade payables' payment period of 41 days.

What is the inventory holding period of the business, in days?

31 days ☐

36 days ☐

46 days ☐

51 days ☐

Task 6.4

A business has a cash operating cycle of 76 days. This is based on an inventory holding period of 65 days, trade receivables' collection period of 55 days and trade payables' payment period of 44 days. The Finance Director of the business wants to improve this.

Which of the following will have the effect of shortening the cash operating cycle of the business?

Taking advantage of early settlement discounts offered by suppliers ☐

Offering an early settlement discount to customers ☐

Increasing the cash balance held in the business's current account ☐

Increasing the credit terms offered to customers from 30 days to 60 days ☐

Task 6.5

A business has an inventory holding period of 45 days, trade receivables' collection period of 40 days and trade payables' payment period of 60 days. The business has launched several new product ranges which will increase the inventory holding period by 9 days and because of the new mix of customers the average receivables' collection period will be 46 days. Supplier payments will be unaffected.

What is the cash operating cycle of the business before and after the planned changes?

Before	After	Tick one
145 days	40 days	
25 days	40 days	
145 days	160 days	
25 days	160 days	

Task 6.6

Select from the picklists to complete the following sentences.

Over-trading can occur when a business has [▼] working capital.

Over-capitalisation occurs when a business has [▼] working capital.

Picklist:

Too much
Too little

··

Task 6.7

You work for a manufacturing company that is facing a short-term liquidity problem. Which of the following assets would you recommend that it sells in order to bridge the cash deficit while doing the minimum damage to its core activities? Explain the reasons for your decision.

1. 10% of its fleet of delivery vehicles

2. Some of its plant and machinery

3. The patent on a new design

4. Its 60% equity stake in the company that supplies a scarce raw material for the manufacturing process

Task 6.8

A company has been expanding very rapidly and has now encountered a liquidity problem, as illustrated by the most recent statement of financial position reproduced below.

Statement of Financial Position extracts

	As at 31 December 20X2 £	As at 31 December 20X1 £
Non-current assets	350,000	270,000
Current assets		
Inventory	200,000	95,000
Receivables	250,000	100,000
Cash	Nil	5,000
	450,000	200,000
Capital and reserves		
Issued share capital	15,000	15,000
Reserves	355,000	335,000
Equity shareholders' funds	370,000	350,000
Current liabilities		
Bank overdraft	200,000	40,000
Trade payables	230,000	80,000
	430,000	120,000

Other information

Sales for the year to 31 December 20X1 were £1.5 million, yielding a gross profit of £300,000, and a net profit before tax of £90,000.

Sales for the year to 31 December 20X2 were £3 million, with a gross profit of £450,000, and net profit before tax of £60,000.

At the beginning of the year to 31 December 20X2 the company bought new manufacturing equipment and recruited six more sales staff.

(a) **Illustrating your answer with figures taken from the question, explain why it is not unusual for manufacturing companies to face a cash shortage when sales are expanding very rapidly.**

(b) **How have the levels of short-term and long-term debt changed between the two years, and what are the dangers of this financing position?**

(c) **Suggest ways in which the company might seek to resolve its current funding problems, and avoid the risks associated with overtrading.**

Chapter 7 – Raising finance

Task 7.1

Are the following statements True or False? Tick the correct box.

Primary banks are those that are involved with the cheque clearing system.

True

False

Secondary banks are also known as commercial banks.

True

False

Task 7.2

What are the four main benefits of financial intermediation?

-
-
-
-

Task 7.3

A bank customer has an overdraft.

Which party is the payable (creditor)? Tick as appropriate.

Bank

Customer

Task 7.4

State six of a bank's main duties to its customer.

-
-
-
-
-
-

Task 7.5

Pravina, an eighteen-year old who lives next door to you, is about to open her first bank account.

Explain to her the rights the bank has in its relationship with her.

Task 7.6

What are the most common reasons underlying a business's identification of a future cash deficit or the need to raise additional finance?

Task 7.7

Which of the following best describe the main features of overdraft finance?

(i)   High interest rate
(ii)   Repayable in instalments
(iii) Useful for capital expenditure
(iv)   Low interest rate
(v)   Short-term form of finance
(vi)   Repayable on demand
(vii) Available as long as required

Tick one option

(i), (ii), (iii)   ☐

(i), (v), (vi)   ☐

(iii), (iv), (vii)   ☐

(ii), (iv), (v)   ☐

Task 7.8

Which of the following best describes the main features of a bank loan?

(i)   High interest rate
(ii)   Repayments can be negotiated
(iii) Useful for capital expenditure
(iv)   Low interest rate
(v)   Short-term form of finance
(vi)   Repayable on demand
(vii) Available as long as required

Tick one option

(i), (ii), (iii)   ☐

(ii), (iv), (vi)   ☐

(i), (v), (vii)   ☐

(ii), (iii), (iv)   ☐

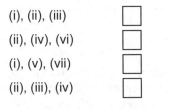

Task 7.9

Both overdraft finance and bank loan finance have various advantages.

Complete the table by entering each of the advantages against the correct type of financing.

Type of finance	Advantages
Overdraft	▼
Bank loan	▼

Picklist:

Relatively low cost
Useful to fund capital expenditure
Precise amount required does not need to be known
Security not normally required
Covenants not normally included
Repayments can be negotiated

Task 7.10

An agricultural business has purchased a new tractor costing £63,800. It has funded the purchase with a medium-term bank loan for the full amount. The business must repay the loan over three years, with monthly payments of £2,380.

Assuming simple interest, calculate the total interest cost (to the nearest £) and the simple annual interest rate (rounded to one decimal place).

Total interest cost (£)	
Simple annual interest rate %	

Task 7.11

A business has applied for a bank loan of £22,500 to purchase some new computers for its head office. The bank requires the loan to be paid off in equal monthly instalments over two and a half years, charging simple interest at 5.25% per annum on the initial loan capital.

What are the monthly payments for the repayments of the capital and the interest on this loan? Round to the nearest pence.

Repayment of capital	
Repayment of interest	

Task 7.12

A bank charges overdraft interest at the rate of 4% per annum.

What is the appropriate interest rate if simple interest is to be applied monthly on the overdrawn balance?

Monthly interest rate (%)	

Task 7.13

A bank loan, which is to be repaid in equal monthly instalments over 3 years, carries a flat rate of interest of 13%.

Choose from the picklists to complete the following sentences.

The APR on the loan would be [▼]

Picklist:

Higher
Lower

Flat rate interest is charged on [▼]

Picklist:

The original capital
The amount of the loan principal outstanding

Task 7.14

A small private limited company requires finance for an expansion project which will require £50,000 of capital expenditure and £10,000 of additional working capital. The finance director has been investigating methods of raising this finance and has found three potential options.

Option 1   A bank loan for £60,000 secured on the non-current assets of the company. The loan is to be repaid in equal instalments over a three-year period and has a fixed rate of interest for the first year of 5%. Thereafter the rate of interest will be variable at 2.5% above the base rate. There will be an arrangement fee for the loan of 0.6% of the bank loan payable at the start of the loan term.

Option 2   The four family directors will all take out a personal secured loan of £15,000 at an annual interest rate of 4%. This money will then be loaned to the company and the personal interest cost for the directors recouped from the company.

Option 3   A bank loan for £50,000 could be taken out secured on the value of the new machinery required for the expansion. The loan will be repaid in equal instalments over five years and the interest is at a fixed rate of 5.5% based upon the outstanding capital balance at the start of the year. An arrangement fee of 0.75% of the bank loan is payable at the beginning of the loan term.

In order to fund the working capital the bank is also offering an overdraft facility of £15,000 which attracts an annual interest rate of 11%. The directors believe that they will require an average overdraft of £8,500 for just the first ten months of the year.

The Articles of Association of the company include the following in respect of the raising of finance:

- Loan finance can be secured on the assets of the company.

- The company must not accept loans from officers or directors of the company.

- The maximum overdraft allowed is £18,000.

- The interest cost to the company of any financing options should be kept as low as possible.

(a) **Complete the table below to calculate the cost to the company for the first year of financing under each of the three options.**

	Arrangement fee	Loan interest £	Overdraft interest £	Total cost £
Option 1				
Option 2				
Option 3				

(b) **Which financial option should the company select taking account of the provisions of the Articles of Association?**

Option 1	
Option 2	
Option 3	
None of the options	

Task 7.15

Famous Ltd is a quoted company which produces a range of branded products, all of which are well-established in their markets, although overall sales have grown by an average of only 2% per annum over the past decade. The board of directors is currently concerned about the company's level of financial gearing. Although the level is not high by industry standards, it is close to breaking the requirements of a loan obtained in 20W2, at a time of high market interest rates. The loan was taken out in order to finance the purchase of land and property, which was used as security for the loan. The loan is repayable in 20X7, with an option to make an early repayment from 20X4.

There are two covenants attaching to the loan, which state:

'At no time shall the ratio of debt capital to shareholders' funds exceed 50%. The company shall also maintain a prudent level of liquidity, defined as a current ratio at no time outside the range of the industry average (as published by the corporate credit analysts, Creditex), plus or minus 20%.'

Famous Ltd's most recent set of accounts is shown in summarised form below. Most of the machinery is only two or three years old, having been purchased mainly using a bank overdraft. The interest rate payable on the bank overdraft is currently 9% pa. The finance director argues that Famous Ltd should take advantage of historically low interest rates on the money markets by issuing a medium-term bond at 5%. Famous Ltd's ordinary shares currently look unattractive compared to comparable companies in the sector which pay out higher dividends compared to the price of the shares. According to the latest published credit assessment by Creditex, the average current ratio for the industry is 1.35.

Summarised financial accounts for the year ended 30 June 20X4

STATEMENT OF FINANCIAL POSITION AS AT 30 JUNE 20X4

	£m	£m
Assets employed		
Non-current (net):		
Land		5.0
Buildings		4.0
Machinery and vehicles		11.0
		20.0
Current:		
Inventory	2.5	
Trade and other receivables	4.0	
Cash	0.5	
		7.0
Total assets		27.0
Financed by:		
Ordinary shares (25p)		5.0
Reserves		10.0
Long-term payables:		
15% Loan notes 20X4-X7		5.0
Current liabilities:		
Payables	4.0	
Bank overdraft	3.0	
		7.0
Total equity and liabilities		27.0

STATEMENT OF PROFIT OR LOSS EXTRACTS FOR THE YEAR ENDED 30 JUNE 20X4

	£m
Revenue	28.00
Profit from operating activities	3.00
Finance costs	(1.00)
Profit before tax	2.00
Tax expense	(0.66)
Profit for the year	1.34
Dividend	(0.70)
Retained profit	0.64

It is now December 20X4.

(a) **Explain and calculate appropriate gearing ratios for Famous Ltd.**

(b) **Assess how close the company is to breaching the loan covenants.**

(c)   **Discuss whether the gearing is in any sense 'dangerous'.**

(d)   **Discuss what financial policies the company might adopt in order to lower its capital gearing and its interest payments.**

Chapter 8 – Managing surplus funds

Task 8.1

Briefly explain the three main factors that should influence any decisions regarding investment of surplus funds.

Task 8.2

A business has £20,000 available to invest in a deposit for 12 months and wishes to achieve a rate of return of 4% per annum.

Which of the following investments would the business accept?

	Will accept ✓
Investment paying interest of £300 every 6 months.	
Investment with a lump sum return of £800 at the end of one year	
Investment paying annual interest of £600 plus a bonus of 1% of the capital invested if the deposit is retained for 1 year	

The business is likely to be able to earn a higher rate of return if the period of time that the capital is available to invest increases.

True ☐

False ☐

If the business wants to be able to withdraw funds on demand this is likely to increase the rate of return available.

True ☐

False ☐

Task 8.3

Which of the following are true about gilt-edged securities?

(i)   They are issued by local authorities.
(ii)   They are variable rate investments.
(iii) The interest is paid twice a year.
(iv)   They are fixed rate investments.
(v)   They are issued by the government.

Tick the correct answer.

(i), (ii), (iii)   ☐

(ii), (iii), (v)   ☐

(iii), (iv), (v)   ☐

(ii), (iv), (v)   ☐

Task 8.4

Interest rates are set to fall in the near future.

What effect will this have on the price of gilt-edged securities? Tick the correct answer.

Their price will rise.   ☐

Their price will fall.   ☐

Task 8.5

A business has £100,000 to invest for a period of approximately six months. Investment in either a bank deposit account or gilt-edged securities is being considered.

What would be the effect of an increase in interest rates on both of these potential investments? Tick the appropriate boxes in the table below.

	Bank deposit	Gilt-edged securities
Increase in value		
Decrease in value		
No effect		

Task 8.6

A business makes a proportion of its sales for cash through a factory outlet.

What security procedures should be adopted for the safe custody of this cash?

Task 8.7

Azrina Ltd manufactures cycles. The company's long-term cash flow forecasts suggests a cash surplus of £1 million will be generated in 20X7 and £1.75 million in 20X8.

The company is considering its future cash management strategy and is examining four business strategies.

For each of the following four strategy scenarios, complete the table to show what action you would take to manage the cash surplus.

(a) No further growth in Azrina Ltd's existing business and no plans for further capital investment

(b) Plans for an acquisition of a cycle parts manufacturer (valued up to £5 million) when a suitable opportunity arises

(c) Development in 20X7 and 20X8 of several new product lines requiring capital investment of £2.5 million

(d) Phased development of two new product lines requiring capital investment of£1.25 million and the intention to acquire another cycle parts manufacturer (value up to £3 million) when a suitable opportunity arises

Possible action	Strategy
Invest in marketable securities	
Spend surplus cash	
Repay surplus cash to owners	
Retain cash for ease of availability	

Task 8.8

A company has produced a cash budget and believes that it will have £50,000 to invest in three months' time. The finance director has identified three possible investment options:

Option 1   Maximum investment £75,000, minimum investment £15,000. Interest rate 1.8% above base rate. 60-day notice period. Low risk and no investment in shares.

Option 2   Minimum investment of £50,000. Interest rate of 2.5%. 90-day notice period. Medium risk and no investment in shares.

Option 3   Minimum investment of £55,000. Interest rate of 3%. 30-day notice period. Low risk and no investment in shares.

The company's treasury policy for investment is as follows:

- Interest rate must be at least 2% above base rate which is currently 0.4%.
- The investment must be convertible into cash within 60 days.
- The investment must be low or medium risk.
- The investment must not include shares.

(a) **Complete the table below to show which of the policy requirements are met by each of the options.**

	Investment of £50,000	Interest 2% above base rate	Convertible within 60 days	Low/medium risk	No shares
Option 1					
Option 2					
Option 3					

(b) **Which option should be selected?**

Option 1	
Option 2	
Option 3	
None of the options	

(c) **Describe the company's appetite for risk with reference to other risk attitudes.**

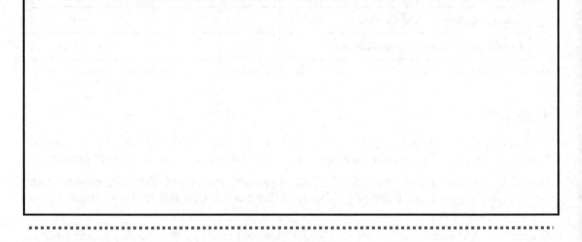

Task 8.9

In the past a company has invested surplus funds in a variety of Treasury stocks and also in fixed term deposits with the bank.

(a) **Selecting from the picklists, complete the following sentences.**

Gilt-edged securities or gilts are [marketable/non-marketable] British Government securities. They pay a [variable/fixed/capped] amount of interest and are available with varying maturity dates which is the date [on which they will be redeemed/they must be kept until].

(b) **If interest rates increase what effect will this have on the interest rate for gilt-edged stocks and a bank deposit account?**

Gilt-edged stocks	Bank deposit account	
Increase	No change	☐
Decrease	No change	☐
No change	Increase	☐
No change	Decrease	☐

(c) **If interest rates increase what effect will this have on the redemption value for gilt-edged stocks and a bank deposit account?**

Gilt-edged stocks	Bank deposit account	
Increase	No change	☐
Decrease	No change	☐
No change	Increase	☐
No change	Decrease	☐

Task 8.10

A company has forecast that it will have surplus funds to invest for a 12 month period. It is considering two investments as follows:

Investment 1

Invest in a bank deposit account that pays compound interest at a variable rate. The current rate of interest on the account is 1.1% per quarter.

Investment 2

Buy a 12 month fixed dated government bond. The bond has a simple interest rate of 2.5% payable every six months.

Explain the advantages AND disadvantages to the company of each of the investments.

You should consider the return offered and the level and type of risk involved with each investment. You should assume that there are no other investments available and that these investments are only available now.

Task 8.11

Why might a company decide to have a treasury department in addition to its finance function, and what would be the main functions of this department?

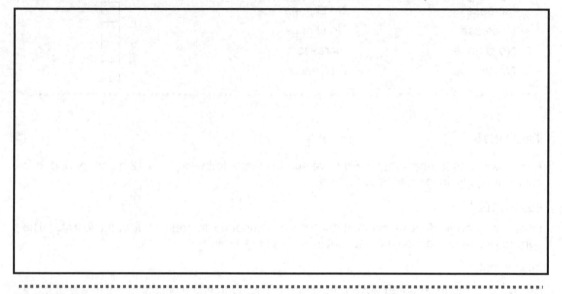

Task 8.12

A company, Selfbuild Ltd, plans to construct a factory and has raised cash through an equity share issue to pay the costs. However, the building of the factory has been delayed and payments will be required three or four months later than expected. Selfbuild Ltd has decided to invest these surplus funds until they are required.

One of the directors of Selfbuild Ltd has identified three possible investment opportunities:

(i)   Treasury bills issued by the central bank. They could be purchased for a period of 91 days. The likely purchase price is £990 per £1,000.

(ii) Equities quoted on the local stock exchange. The stock exchange has had a good record recently with the equity index increasing in value for 14 consecutive months. The director recommends investment in three large multinational companies with a history of paying an annual dividend that provides an annual yield of 10% on the current share price.

(iii) The company's bank would pay 3.5% per year on money placed in a deposit account with 30 day's notice.

Prepare notes for the director on the risk and effective return of each of the above investment opportunities and recommend which is most suitable for Selfbuild Ltd.

Answer bank

Answer bank

Chapter 1

Task 1.1

If a business makes a profit this means that │ its revenue is greater than its expenses. │

Cash flow and profit will │ not normally │ be the same figure for a period.

....

Task 1.2

1   Accruals accounting
2   Non-cash expenses
3   Capital introduced or dividends/drawings paid
4   Purchase of non-current assets
5   Sale of non-current assets

....

Task 1.3

	£'000
Sales receipts	820
Purchase payments	575
Overhead payments	95

Workings

Sales receipts	=	860 + 45 – 85	=	820
Purchase payments	=	600 + 75 – 100	=	575
Overhead payments	=	100 + 40 – 45	=	95

....

Task 1.4

The correct answer is: £39,500

The carrying amount of non-current assets increased by £27,000 but this was after deducting £12,500 of depreciation, so the cash paid for new assets must have been £27,000 + £12,500 = £39,500.

....

Task 1.5

The correct answer is: £1,960 loss

The carrying amount of the machine at the date of disposal is £25,760 (64,400 – 38,640). If it is sold for £23,800, it must have been sold at a loss of £1,960 (23,800 – 25,760).

....

Task 1.6

The correct answer is: £91,500

The carrying amount of the building at the date of disposal is £56,500 (105,000 – 48,500). If it is sold for a profit of £35,000, it must have been sold for more than its carrying amount, so the cash proceeds are £56,500 + £35000 = £91,500.

....

Task 1.7

Sales Ledger Control Account			
	Dr £		Cr £
Opening trade receivables	34,500		
Sales revenue per statement of profit or loss	252,000	Cash received	238,600
		Closing trade receivables	47,900
	286,500		286,500

....

Chapter 2

Task 2.1

Week	Day	Takings £	Five-day moving average £
1	Monday	1,260	
	Tuesday	1,600	
	Wednesday	1,630	1,620
	Thursday	1,780	1,636
	Friday	1,830	1,666
2	Monday	1,340	1,668
	Tuesday	1,750	1,682
	Wednesday	1,640	1,712
	Thursday	1,850	1,754
	Friday	1,980	1,736
3	Monday	1,550	1,732
	Tuesday	1,660	1,736
	Wednesday	1,620	1,734
	Thursday	1,870	
	Friday	1,970	

Task 2.2

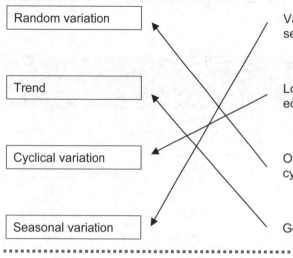

Random variation → Variations in the time series due to the seasonality of the business

Trend → Long-term variations caused by general economic factors

Cyclical variation → Other variations not due to the trend, cyclical or seasonal variations

Seasonal variation → General movement in the time series figure

Task 2.3

(a)

	Sales volume	Trend	Monthly variation (volume less trend)
	Units	Units	Units
January	20,000		
February	17,400	17,900	–500
March	16,300	18,700	–2,400
April	22,400	19,500	2,900
May	19,800	20,300	–500
June	18,700	21,100	–2,400
July	24,800	21,900	2,900
August	22,200	22,700	–500
September	21,100	23,500	–2,400
October	27,200	24,300	2,900
November	24,600	25,100	–500
December	23,500		

The monthly sales volume trend is ⎕ 800 ⎕ units.

(**Working:** (25,100 – 17,900)/9 changes in trend)

(b) The variation for January is not given. However the variations can be seen to repeat and sum to zero on a quarterly basis (–500, –2400, +2900). Thus the variation for December would be –2400 and that for January +2900.

	Forecast trend Units	Variation Units	Forecast sales volume Units
January (25,100 + (2 × 800))	26,700	2,900	29,600
February (25,100 + (3 × 800))	27,500	–500	27,000
March (25,100 + (4 × 800))	28,300	–2,400	25,900

Task 2.4

Average increase in trend value $= \dfrac{(9,705 - 7,494)}{11}$

$\qquad\qquad = 201$ units

Future trend values

Quarter 1 (9,705 + 201) 9,906 units
Quarter 2 (9,705 + (2 × 201)) 10,107 units
Quarter 3 (9,705 + (3 × 201)) 10,308 units
Quarter 4 (9,705 + (4 × 201)) 10,509 units

Quarter	Trend forecast	Average seasonal variation	Forecast of actual sales units	Forecast revenue £
1	9,906	+53	9,959	448,155
2	10,107	+997	11,104	499,680
3	10,308	+1,203	11,511	517,995
4	10,509	–2,253	8,256	371,520

Task 2.5

	£
January sales 21,000 × £30 × 60%	378,000
February sales 22,000 × £30 × 1.04 × 40%	274,560
Total March receipts	**652,560**

Task 2.6

The correct answer is: £355,729

March cash outflow for overheads   = £347,000 × 1.0125 × 1.0125

                                             = £355,729

Task 2.7

	£
December	2.60 × 169.0/166.3 = £2.64
January	2.60 × 173.4/166.3 = £2.71
February	2.60 × 177.2/166.3 = £2.77

Task 2.8

Forecast P12 sales = ((27 × 12) – 24) × 1.35 = 405 units

Task 2.9

What is the principal budget factor?

Known as the key budget factor or limiting budget factor, this is the factor which, at any given time, effectively limits the activities of an organisation. The principal budget factor is usually sales demand: a company is usually restricted from making and selling more of its products because there would be no sales demand for the increased output at a price which would be acceptable/profitable for the company. The principal budget factor may also be machine capacity, distribution and selling resources, the availability of key raw materials or the availability of cash.

The importance of the principal budget factor

Once this factor is identified then the rest of the budget can be prepared. For example, if sales are the principal budget factor then the production budget can only be prepared after the sales budget is complete.

Sales forecasting

There are two basic approaches to sales forecasting:

(i) Use of internal estimates

In-house sales staff can forecast future sales using their experience and knowledge and by considering the following factors:

(1) Past sales figures
(2) Economic environment
(3) Competitor actions

(ii) Statistical techniques

Statistical techniques are most appropriate if past sales patterns give some indication of future sales patterns or there is correlation between two factors – that is there is a relationship between two variables.

Using historical data – a time series, and analysing these figures, the patterns and relationships can be determined and used to predict future performance.

The time series has four components:

*   Trend (the general movement of the figures)
*   Cyclical variation (due to general economic conditions)
*   Seasonal variation (due to the time of year, month or other time period)
*   Random variation (due to unpredictable events)

The techniques that can be used include regression analysis by the least squares method in combination with moving averages analysis.

Task 2.10

(a) For time period 33, x = 33

If y = 10,000 + 4,200x, then y = 148,600

Time period 33 is a first quarter and so the seasonal variation index value is 120.

Forecast = 148,600 × 1.2 = 178,320

(b) The problems of extrapolating past performance into the future stem from the assumptions made in such extrapolations.

(i) External conditions are assumed to remain unchanged. This can make extrapolated data invalid. For example, changes in the rate of sales tax (such as VAT) may affect sales prices and so the pattern of demand in the future.

(ii) The relationship between the variables is assumed to be linear. For example, it may be assumed that if sales volume doubles then variable cost will also double. This may have been true for activity levels experienced in the past but it may not be valid to assume that the relationship will hold for activity levels in the future.

(iii) It is assumed that all variables affecting past performance have been identified and that other conditions have remained constant. The identified variables may not be the only factors affecting performance and the omission of other valid variables will affect the accuracy of the extrapolation.

These problems do not mean that the extrapolation of past performance into the future has no value. It is important that the resulting forecast is used with caution, however. Anyone relying on the forecast as the basis for decision making must be aware of its shortcomings and of any assumptions on which it is based.

Chapter 3

Task 3.1

Type of receipt/payment	Example
Regular revenue receipts	Income received from the operating activities of the business which are expected to occur frequently
Regular revenue payments	Payments due to the operating activities of the business that are expected to be incurred frequently
Exceptional receipts/payments	Income received from HM Revenue and Customs
	Income received from the operating activities of the business which are not expected to occur frequently
	Payments due to the operating activities of the business that are not expected to be incurred frequently
Capital payments/receipts	Income that arises from the proceeds of the sale of non-current assets
	Payments that arise from the acquisition of non-current assets
	Income received from the owner of the business
Drawings/dividends	Payments made to the owner of the business

Task 3.2

	October £	November £	December £
Cash sales			
October 280,000 × 30%	84,000		
November 250,000 × 30%		75,000	
December 220,000 × 30%			66,000
Credit sales			
August 240,000 × 30%	72,000		
September 265,000 × 40%	106,000		
September 265,000 × 30%		79,500	
October 280,000 × 40%		112,000	
October 280,000 × 30%			84,000
November 250,000 × 40%			100,000
Total cash receipts	**262,000**	**266,500**	**250,000**

Task 3.3

	October £	November £	December £
August 180,000 × 35%	63,000		
September 165,000 × 45%	74,250		
September 165,000 × 35%		57,750	
October 190,000 × 20% × 98%	37,240		
October 190,000 × 45%		85,500	
October 190,000 × 35%			66,500
November 200,000 × 20% × 98%		39,200	
November 200,000 × 45%			90,000
December 220,000 × 20% × 98%			43,120
Total cash payments	**174,490**	**182,450**	**199,620**

Task 3.4

		January £	February £	March £
Purchases		22,000	24,000	26,000
Cash sales = Purchases × 150%		33,000	36,000	39,000

The margin that the retailer is making is 33.33%.

(**Working:** January profit is £11,000 (£33,000 – £22,000), so profit margin = 11,000/33,000 = 33.33%)

Task 3.5

(a)

	April £	May £	June £
March sales 650,000 × 70%	455,000		
April sales 600,000 × 25% × 97%	145,500		
April sales 600,000 × 70%		420,000	
May sales 580,000 × 25% × 97%		140,650	
May sales 580,000 × 70%			406,000
June sales 550,000 × 25% × 97%			133,375
Total cash receipts	**600,500**	**560,650**	**539,375**

(b)

	April £	May £	June £
March sales 650,000 × 70%	455,000		
April sales 600,000 × 30% × 95%	171,000		
April sales 600,000 × 70%		420,000	
May sales 580,000 × 30% × 95%		165,300	
May sales 580,000 × 70%			406,000
June sales 550,000 × 30% × 95%			156,750
Total cash receipts	**626,000**	**585,300**	**562,750**

Task 3.6

(a) Closing receivables = 290,510/365 × 49 = £39,000

Cash received is therefore:

	£
Opening receivables	22,000
Credit sales	290,510
Closing receivables	(39,000)
Cash received	273,510

(b) Sales revenue for the year net of irrecoverable debts = £492,750 × 95% = £468,112.50. (Alternative approach: Irrecoverable debts for the year = 5% × £492,750 = £24,637.50. Hence sales revenue that will actually be collected in cash = £492,750 – £24,637.50 = £468,112.50)

Closing receivables at year end (net of irrecoverable debts) = £468,112.50 × 60/365 = £76,950. (Alternative calculation = £492,750 × 60/365 × 95% = £76,950)

Expected cash receipts = opening receivables + sales revenue during the year – closing receivables

= £83,000 + £468,112.50 – £76,950

= £474,162.50

Task 3.7

	Period 1	Period 2
	£'000	£'000
Sales receipts (W1)	5,144	5,314
Raw materials purchases (W2)	(2,139)	(2,201)
Production wages (W3)	(1,720)	(1,722)
Variable production expenses (production units × £1.10)	(231)	(231)
Variable selling expenses (sales units × £1.60)	(240)	(320)
Fixed production expenses (W4)	(1,376)	0
Interest (W5)	0	(450)
Net cash flow for the period	(562)	390
Opening cash balance	76	(486)
Closing cash balance	(486)	(96)

Workings

Working 1

Sales

	Period 1	Period 2
	£'000	£'000
Sales (150,000 × £30 and 200,000 × £30)	4,500	6,000
Irrecoverable debts @ 2%	(90)	(120)
Net sales	4,410	5,880
Opening trade receivables	2,430	1,696
Closing trade receivables*	(1,696)	(2,262)
Receipts	5,144	5,314

* Net sales × 5/13 = 1,696

Working 2

Materials

	Period 1	Period 2
	£'000	£'000
Production (210,000 × £9.50)	1,995	1,995
Closing inventory	921*	1,125*
Opening inventory	(710)	(921)
Purchases	2,206	2,199
Opening payables	612	679
Closing payables	(679)**	(677)**
Paid	2,139	2,201

* 1,995 × 6/13 (Period 1) and 220 × £9.50 × 7/13 (Period 2)

** 2,206 × 4/13 (Period 1) and 2,199 × 4/13 (Period 2)

Working 3

Production wages

	Period 1	Period 2
	£'000	£'000
Production (210 × £8.20/unit)	1,722	1,722
Opening unpaid wages	130	132
Closing unpaid wages (£1,722/13)	(132)	(132)
Paid	1,720	1,722

Working 4

Other fixed production expenses = 860,000 units × £3.20 = £2,752,000

Paid in period 1 = £2,752,000/2 = £1,376,000

Note: ignore depreciation as it is a non-cash expense.

Working 5

Annual interest = £10,000,000 × 9% = £900,000.

Paid in period 2 = £900,000/2 = £450,000

Chapter 4

Task 4.1

(a) The correct answer is Y only.

Workings:

Cost of not taking discount (and therefore taking credit from the supplier) =

$$\left(\frac{100}{100-d}\right)^{\frac{12}{m}} \text{ where } d = \% \text{ discount,}$$

m = reduction in payment period in months necessary to achieve discount

Cost of taking credit from X = $\left(\frac{100}{97}\right)^{4} - 1 = 12.96\%$

Cost of taking credit from Y = $\left(\frac{100}{96}\right)^{3} - 1 = 13.02\%$

Thus it is cheaper to use the overdraft at a cost of 13% to fund immediate payment to Y, whereas it is better to take credit from X for 3 months.

(Note that the formula here uses months because this is how the settlement period is expressed but can be changed if the settlement terms are expressed in days – see below.)

(b) Cost of early settlement discount is estimated using the formula

$$= \left(\frac{100}{100-d}\right)^{\frac{365}{t}} - 1$$

$$= \left(\frac{100}{100-2.5}\right)^{\frac{365}{65-15}} - 1$$

$$= \left(\frac{100}{97.5}\right)^{7.3} - 1$$

$$= 20.3\%$$

(c) Evaluation of change in credit policy

Current average collection period	= 40 days
Current accounts receivable	= £4m × 40/365
	= £438,356
Average collection period under new policy	= (25% × 10 days) + (75% × 50 days)
	= 40 days
New level of credit sales	= £4m × 1.08
	= £4.32m
Accounts receivable after policy change	= £4.32m × 40/365
	= £473,425
Increase in financing cost	= £(473,425 – 438,356) × 5%
	= £1,753

	£
Increase in financing cost	1,753
Incremental costs (£4.32m × 1%)	43,200
Sales revenue foregone due to discount (25% × £4.32m × 2%)	21,600
Increase in costs	66,553
Contribution from increased sales (£4m × 8% × 50%)	160,000
Net benefit of policy change	93,447

The proposed policy will therefore increase profitability.

Task 4.2

(a) Purchases budget

	April kgs	May kgs	June kgs	July kgs
Materials required for production				
April 1,220 × 2 kg	2,440			
May 1,320 × 2 kg		2,640		
June 1,520 × 2 kg			3,040	
July 1,620 × 2 kg				3,240
Opening inventory	– 550	– 500	– 450	– 400
Closing inventory	500	450	400	350
Purchases in kgs	2,390	2,590	2,990	3,190

	April £	May £	June £	July £
April 2,390 × £40	95,600			
May 2,590 × £40		103,600		
June 2,990 × £40			119,600	
July 3,190 × £40				127,600

(b) **Cash payments to suppliers for May to July**

	May £	June £	July £
Cash payments	95,600	103,600	119,600

....

Task 4.3

Labour budget – hours	April Hours	May Hours	June Hours
April 7,050/3	2,350		
May 6,450/3		2,150	
June 6,000/3			2,000
Labour budget – £	April £	May £	June £
April 2,350 × £8.40	19,740		
May 2,150 × £8.40		18,060	
June 2,000 × £8.40			16,800

....

Task 4.4

(a) Cash receipts from customers

		July £	August £	September £
April sales	420,000 × 12%	50,400		
May sales	400,000 × 25%	100,000		
	400,000 × 12%		48,000	
June sales	480,000 × 40%	192,000		
	480,000 × 25%		120,000	
	480,000 × 12%			57,600
July sales	500,000 × 20% × 96%	96,000		
	500,000 × 40%		200,000	
	500,000 × 25%			125,000
August sales	520,000 × 20% × 96%		99,840	
	520,000 × 40%			208,000
September sales	510,000 × 20% × 96%			97,920
Total receipts		**438,400**	**467,840**	**488,520**

(b) Cash payments to suppliers

		July £	August £	September £
May purchases	250,000 × 60%	150,000		
June purchases	240,000 × 40%	96,000		
	240,000 × 60%		144,000	
July purchases	280,000 × 40%		112,000	
	280,000 × 60%			168,000
August purchases	300,000 × 40%			120,000
Total payments		**246,000**	**256,000**	**288,000**

(c) **Cash payments for general overheads**

		July £	August £	September £
June overheads	(50,000 – 6,000) × 25%	11,000		
July overheads	(50,000 – 6,000) × 75%	33,000		
	(50,000 – 6,000) × 25%		11,000	
August overheads	(55,000 – 6,000) × 75%		36,750	
	(55,000 – 6,000) × 25%			12,250
September overheads	(55,000 – 6,000) × 75%			36,750
Total overhead payments		**44,000**	**47,750**	**49,000**

(d) **Cash budget – July to September**

	July £	August £	September £
Receipts			
Receipts from credit sales	438,400	467,840	488,520
Proceeds from sale of equipment	0	7,500	0
Total receipts	**438,400**	**475,340**	**488,520**
Payments			
Payments to suppliers	–246,000	–256,000	–288,000
Wages	–60,000	–60,000	–60,000
Overheads	–44,000	–47,750	–49,000
Selling expenses	–48,000	–50,000	–52,000
Equipment	0	–42,000	0
Overdraft interest	–820	–424	–233
Total payments	**–398,820**	**–456,174**	**–449,233**
Net cash flow	39,580	19,166	39,287
Opening balance	–82,000	–42,420	–23,254
Closing balance	**–42,420**	**–23,254**	**16,033**

Task 4.5

(a) Cash receipts from sales

		October £	November £	December £
August sales	5,000 × £75 × 60%	225,000		
September sales	5,100 × £75 × 40%	153,000		
	5,100 × £75 × 60%		229,500	
October sales	5,400 × £75 × 40%		162,000	
	5,400 × £75 × 60%			243,000
November sales	5,800 × £75 × 40%			174,000
Total cash receipts		**378,000**	**391,500**	**417,000**

(b) Purchases budget

	Aug kg	Sept kg	Oct kg	Nov kg
Kgs required for production Production × 3 kg	15,300	16,500	17,700	18,300
Opening inventory	– 3,000	– 3,000	– 3,000	– 3,200
Closing inventory	3,000	3,000	3,200	3,500
Purchases in kgs	**15,300**	**16,500**	**17,900**	**18,600**
	£	£	£	£
Purchases in £ Kgs × £9	**137,700**	**148,500**	**161,100**	**167,400**

(c) Payments to suppliers

		Oct £	Nov £	Dec £
August purchases	137,700 × 40%	55,080		
September purchases	148,500 × 60%	89,100		
	148,500 × 40%		59,400	
October purchases	161,100 × 60%		96,660	
	161,100 × 40%			64,440
November purchases	167,400 × 60%			100,440
Total cash payments		**144,180**	**156,060**	**164,880**

(d) Labour budget

	Oct Hours	Nov Hours	Dec Hours
Production × 3 hours	16,500	17,700	18,300
	£	£	£
Production hours × £7.20	118,800	127,440	131,760

(e) Cash budget – October to December

	October £	November £	December £
Receipts			
From credit customers	**378,000**	**391,500**	**417,000**
Payments			
To credit suppliers	−144,180	−156,060	−164,880
Wages	−118,800	−127,440	−131,760
Production overheads	−50,000	−50,000	−50,000
General overheads	−60,000	−60,000	−68,000
Total payments	**−372,980**	**−393,500**	**−414,640**
Net cash flow	5,020	−2,000	2,360
Opening bank balance	40,000	45,020	43,020
Closing bank balance	**45,020**	**43,020**	**45,380**

Task 4.6

(a) Payments to suppliers with no settlement discount

		October £	November £	December £
August purchases	520,000 × 40%	208,000		
September purchases	550,000 × 60%	330,000		
	550,000 × 40%		220,000	
October purchases	560,000 × 60%		336,000	
	560,000 × 40%			224,000
November purchases	580,000 × 60%			348,000
Total cash payments		**538,000**	**556,000**	**572,000**

(b) Payments to suppliers with settlement discount

		October £	November £	December £
August purchases	520,000 × 40%	208,000		
September purchases	550,000 × 60%	330,000		
	550,000 × 40%		220,000	
October purchases	560,000 × 30% × 97%	162,960		
	560,000 × 40%		224,000	
	560,000 × 30%			168,000
November purchases	580,000 × 30% × 97%		168,780	
	580,000 × 40%			232,000
December purchases	600,000 × 30% × 97%			174,600
Total cash payments		**700,960**	**612,780**	**574,600**

Task 4.7

(a)

	April £	May £	June £
Original value of forecast sales (£1 per unit)	140,000	150,000	155,000
Original timing of receipts	140,000	176,000	144,000
Revised value of forecast sales (£0.90 per unit)	126,000	135,000	139,500
Revised timing of receipts	140,000	170,400	129,600
Increase/(decrease) in sales receipts	**0**	**(5,600)**	**(14,400)**

Working

Original timing of receipts

May   120,000 + (40% × 140,000) = 176,000
June   (60% × 140,000) + (40% × 150,000) = 144,000

Revised timing of receipts

May   120,000 + (40% × 126,000) = 170,400
June   (60% × 126,000) + (40% × 135,000) = 129,600

(b)

	April £	May £	June £
Original net cash flow	− 12,000	40,000	44,000
Increase/(decrease) in sales receipts per (a)	0	− 5,600	− 14,400
Revised net cash flow	− 12,000	34,400	29,600
Opening bank balance	− 20,000	− 32,000	2,400
Closing bank balance	− 32,000	2,400	32,000

Task 4.8

(a) The basic approach of sensitivity analysis is to calculate the outcomes under alternative assumptions to determine how sensitive the company's plans are to changing conditions. In the context of a cash budget, the cash flows will change if the assumptions used to formulate the budget are altered.

One approach is to develop a range of possibilities under different assumptions (eg what if the sales price is discounted by 2%, 5%, 10% respectively) and use this to prepare alternative cash budgets. Another is to measure how sensitive the budget is to changes in certain variables by calculating the impact of a particular change and comparing the original and revised cash flows. Sensitivity analysis can thus be used to assess which assumptions have the biggest impact on the budget.

It is also important to recognise that changes in one assumption may affect opther variables. Here, a discount in the sales price, which by itself would have a negative impact on cash receipts may encourage more customers and hence give rise to an overall increase in sales volumes.

(b) Contribution = £3.00 − £1.65 = £1.35

(i) **Sensitivity to sales volume**

For profit of zero, contribution has to decrease by £7,000. This represents a reduction in sales of £7,000/(20,000 units × £1.35) = 25.93%

(ii) **Sensitivity to sales price**

For a profit of zero, contribution has to decrease by £7,000. This represents a reduction in selling price of 7,000/(20,000 × £3.00) = 11.67%

(iii) **Sensitivity to variable costs**

For a profit of zero, contribution has to decrease by £7,000. This represents an increase in variable costs of 7,000/(20,000 × £1.65) = 21.21%

Task 4.9

(a) Output tax   = £2,125,000 × 20% = £425,000

Input tax   = £1,975,000 × 20% = £395,000

Amount due to HMRC = output tax less input tax = £425,000 – £395,000 = £30,000

(b) One month and 7 days after the end of the relevant VAT period

Chapter 5

Task 5.1

	Budget £	Actual £	Variance £	Adv/Fav £
Receipts:				
Cash sales receipts	101,000	94,000	7,000	Adv
Credit sales receipts	487,000	475,000	12,000	Adv
Total receipts	588,000	569,000	19,000	Adv
Payments:				
Credit suppliers	303,000	294,000	9,000	Fav
Wages	155,000	162,000	7,000	Adv
Variable overheads	98,600	99,400	800	Adv
Fixed overheads	40,000	40,000	0	
Capital expenditure	0	45,000	45,000	Adv
Total payments	596,600	640,400	43,800	Adv
Net cash flow	– 8,600	– 71,400	62,800	Adv
Balance b/f	20,300	20,300	0	
Balance c/f	11,700	– 51,100	62,800	Adv

Task 5.2

(a)

	£
Budgeted closing bank balance	61,900
Surplus in cash sales	13,000
Shortfall in credit sales receipts	– 25,000
Increase in proceeds from sales from non-current assets	22,000
Increase in payments to credit suppliers	– 35,000
No change in wages	0

	£
Increase in variable overheads	– 7,400
Increase in fixed overheads	– 2,000
Increase in purchase of non-current assets	– 46,000
No change in dividend payments	0
Actual closing bank balance	– 18,500

(b) Delay capital expenditure

Although the other options may have resulted in a lower overdraft it is unlikely that any of these on their own are sufficient to reduce the deficit by £18,500.

Task 5.3

(a)

	Budget February £	Actual February £	Variance £
Cash receipts			
Receipts from sales	148,800	145,600	−3,200
Deposit account interest	100	100	-
Total cash receipts	**148,900**	**145,700**	**−3,200**
Cash payments			
Payments to suppliers	−41,600	−56,000	−14,400
Salaries	−43,000	−45,150	−2,150
Administration overheads	−30,000	−30,000	-
Capital expenditure	−20,000	−6,000	+14,000
Total payments	**−134,600**	**−137,150**	**−2,550**
Net cash flow	**14,300**	**8,550**	**−5,750**
Opening cash balance	−25,900	−25,900	-
Closing cash balance	**−11,600**	**−17,350**	**−5,750**

(b)

	£
Budgeted closing bank balance	−11,600
Shortfall in sales receipts	−3,200
No change in deposit account interest	0
Increase in payments to credit suppliers	−14,400
Increase in salaries	−2,150
No change in administration overheads	0
Decrease in capital expenditure	+14,000
Actual closing bank balance	−17,350

(c)

Sales receipts	Loss of customers

Payments to suppliers	Increase in suppliers prices

Salaries	Bonus paid to staff

Capital expenditure	Negotiated credit with supplier of equipment, provided initial deposit paid in month of purchase

....

Task 5.4

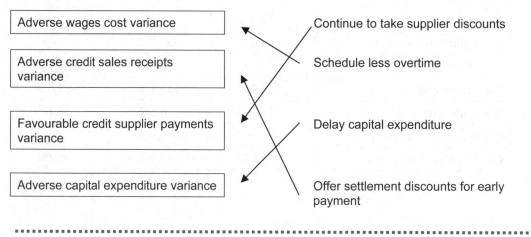

Adverse wages cost variance — Schedule less overtime

Adverse credit sales receipts variance — Offer settlement discounts for early payment

Favourable credit supplier payments variance — Continue to take supplier discounts

Adverse capital expenditure variance — Delay capital expenditure

....

Task 5.5

(a) | £ 26,300 |

Budgeted overhead = £27,500 – 1,200 = £26,300

(b) | £20,300 |

Budgeted cost of non-current asset = £18,000 + £2,300 = £20,300

Task 5.6

(a)

	Budget	Actual	Variance	Adv/Fav
Sales (units)	72,000	64,000	8,000	Adv
Cash received	£720,000	£430,080	289,920	Adv
Selling price	£10 per unit	£8.40 per unit	1.60	Adv

(b) Possible causes of variances:

(i) Stronger than anticipated **competition** forced prices down.

(ii) A **reduction** in the overall levels of **demand** resulted in a reduction in sales volume and a downward pressure on prices.

(iii) Cash received is lower than the sales revenue (64,000 units × £8.40 = £537,600), which indicates that not all the money was received from the sales. Strong competition may have lead to the company offering credit terms to customers, which was not budgeted for.

(iv) Poor planning techniques may have meant that the original budget was not realistic.

(c) Analysing the variances will assist the company do the following:

Improve future planning – any non-controllable variances will need to be factored in to future plans so that the company can make decisions based on sound financial information.

Control performance – if the reasons for the variances are controllable then the company can make changes to come in on budget in future periods.

Performance management – the management of resources is a key indication of performance and so variances can be used as one method of assessing the performance of managers.

(d) Factors to be considered before deciding to investigate a variance.

Size of variance – Small variations in a single period are bound to occur and are unlikely to be significant. Obtaining an 'explanation' is likely to be time-consuming and irritating for the manager concerned. The explanation will often be 'chance', which is not, in any case, particularly helpful. For such variations further investigation is not worthwhile.

Controllability – Controllability must also influence the decision whether to investigate further. If there is a general worldwide price increase in the price of an important raw material there is nothing that can be done internally to control the effect of this. Uncontrollable variances call for a change in the plan, not an investigation into the past.

Variance trend – Caution should be exercised before investigating a 'snapshot' variance in too much detail. For example, an adverse variance in Month 1 could indicate that control action is needed, but in a large company with many processes to monitor, it may be advisable to postpone direct action until the variances for subsequent months have been analysed. If they show a favourable trend then intervention will not be necessary.

You only need to discuss three factors but your answer may also have included the following.

Cost – The likely cost of an investigation needs to be weighed against the cost to the organisation of allowing the variance to continue in future periods.

Interrelationship of variances – Quite possibly, individual variances should not be looked at in isolation. One variance might be inter-related with another, and much of it might have occurred only because the other, inter-related, variance occurred too. When two variances are interdependent (interrelated) one will usually be adverse and the other one favourable.

Task 5.7

Variance analysis compares the actual effects of a business' operations to those that were anticipated in the business plans.

The business environment

Variance analysis assumes that the future is predictable. The current business environment is more dynamic and liable to change than it was in the past, so the use of variance analysis for planning and control purposes is not always ideal.

Non financial targets

Variance analysis concentrates on a **narrow range of costs** only and does not give sufficient attention to non-financial issues such as quality and customer satisfaction. For example, an aggressive credit control approach could result in a good cash flow position, but negatively impact customer goodwill and repeat sales.

Responsibility for variances

Standard costing systems make **individual managers responsible** for the variances relating to their part of the organisation's activities. Modern manufacturing techniques aim to make **all personnel** aware of, and responsible for, the importance of supplying the customer with a quality product.

Despite the arguments set out above, standard costing and variance analysis can be relevant in the modern manufacturing environment for the following reasons.

Planning. Even in a dynamic environment, budgets will still need to be quantified. The organisation needs to know what cash flow it expects in order to make enough working capital available to cover the immediate costs of the business.

Control. Changes from plan will still be relevant to performance management. Cash is a vital element of any business and therefore it is an important management role to compare the actual cash flows for a period to the expected cash flows as shown in the cash flow forecast. Variance analysis can be to used for example to identify and control trade receivables from increasing, or prevent trade payables being paid too quickly.

Chapter 6

Task 6.1

The cash operating cycle time is the	inventory holding period plus trade receivables' collection period less trade payables' payment period.
Liquid assets include	cash and short-term investments.

Task 6.2

The correct answer is: 4 months

	Months
Raw material inventory holding period	4.0
Less credit taken from suppliers	(3.0)
Finished goods inventory holding period	1.0
Trade receivables' collection period	2.0
Cash operating cycle	4.0

Task 6.3

The correct answer is: 51 days

Working:

	Days
Inventory holding period	51
Trade receivables' collection period	77
	128
Less trade payables' payment period	(41)
Cash operating cycle	87

Task 6.4

The correct answer is: Offering an early settlement discount to customers

Offering an early settlement discount to customers will hopefully encourage customers to pay earlier. This will have the effect of reducing the trade receivables' collection period, which will in turn reduce the cash operating cycle of the business.

Task 6.5

The correct answer is:

25 days	40 days	✓

Working:

	Before	After
Inventory holding period	45	54
Trade receivables' collection period	40	46
Trade payables' payment period	60	60
Cash operating cycle	45 + 40 – 60 = 25	54 + 46 – 60 = 40

Task 6.6

Over-trading can occur when a business has | too little | working capital.

Over-capitalisation occurs when a business has | too much | working capital.

Task 6.7

The company should sell 10% of its delivery vehicles. It will keep the majority of its delivery vehicles, and it is safe to assume that reasonably priced alternatives are available. This sale should not damage the long term profitability of the company.

Assuming that the plant and machinery is in use and not redundant, selling this would impact a core activity of the business. In addition the likely sale proceeds may not reflect the actual value in use to the business. The plant should not be sold in these circumstances.

The patent is likely to be a key to securing the long-term future profitability of the company. It should not be sold to meet short-term needs as this will damage the company's competitive advantage.

A 60% stake constitutes a controlling interest in the supplier. Given that this supplier provides a scarce raw material to the company, selling this shareholding could damage the supply of this raw material.

Task 6.8

(a) Manufacturing companies generally have a relatively long operating cycle and a correspondingly large working capital requirement. When the level of sales increases, there is an increased investment in:

   (i) Inventory, as additional raw materials are purchased to produce the additional goods.

   (ii) Staff costs, both direct in production, and indirect in sales and credit control overhead.

   (iii) Receivables since most manufacturing companies sell on credit, and additional sales will therefore translate into a higher level of receivables.

   Need for working capital investment

   The company may also need to purchase equipment to increase its capacity. All of these areas require an immediate investment of cash, in advance of the cash flow benefits of the additional sales and operating profits being felt. Although the company may also benefit from an increased level of payables, this will not be enough to offset the other factors, and therefore additional cash will be required to finance this process.

   This problem can be illustrated using the figures from the company.

   (i) During the last year, sales have doubled by from £1.5m to £3m.

   (ii) There has been additional net investment of £80,000 in non-current assets during the same period.

   (iii) The level of inventory has more than doubled from £95,000 to £200,000.

   (iv) Receivables have increased by £150,000 from £100,000 to £250,000, an increase of 150%.

   (v) Six additional sales staff have been recruited.

   These changes have resulted in a massive increase in the bank overdraft of £160,000 from £40,000 to £200,000, (£165,000 if the £5,000 cash balance in 20X1 is included) and in the level of trade payables, which has nearly trebled from £80,000 to £230,000.

   The cash resources at the start of the year were only £5,000, and the increased level of trading has been financed entirely from short-term bank borrowings and trade payables.

(b) Increase in debt levels

   It has been seen that there has been a large increase in the level of short-term borrowings in the form of bank loans and trade payables. The ratio of equity: bank debt has fallen from 8.75 times (£350,000 ÷ £40,000) to 1.85 times (£370,000 ÷ £200,000), and the real level of reliance on debt is even higher if the increase in the level of trade payables is taken into account. The company has financed its expansion wholly by using short-term debt.

Dangers of financing position

(i)   Lack of matching

The company should match long-term assets with long-term funds. At present, both the increase in working capital and the increase in non-current assets are being financed out of short-term debt.

(ii) Exceeding terms of trade

Although the use of trade payables as a source of finance is attractive because there is rarely any interest charge, it is likely that the company is exceeding its terms of trade, since the increase in the level of payables is so much greater than the increase in the level of sales. It is therefore running the risk of losing the goodwill of its suppliers.

(iii) Inability to obtain credit

The current state of the funding means that, on the basis of the statement of financial position, the company may find it hard to obtain additional credit from existing or new suppliers. This is because of the high level of financial risk now being carried by the trade payables who have no security for their credit.

(iv) Problems with bank

There is no information on the nature of any agreements that the company has with the bank over funding, or any indication as to the size of the overdraft limit. However, as the level of short-term funding increases, the bank will want to review the current and forecast trading situation with the company before increasing its stake in the company any further. It would be in the interest of both parties if the existing overdraft were replaced with some form of secured medium-term bank debt.

(c) The main needs of the company are to reduce its reliance on short-term debt and to ease its current cash shortage. This could be achieved in the following ways.

(i)   Conversion of loan

The short-term bank loan could be converted to a longer-term loan or debenture.

(ii) Increase equity

The company could seek to increase the level of equity investment, which would reduce the level of gearing to a safer level.

(iii) Improved inventory and receivable control

As has already been shown, certain elements of working capital have increased at a faster rate than the sales growth would appear to warrant. In particular, there appears to be scope for improving the control of inventory and receivables. If both these elements were restricted in line with the growth in sales, this would release working capital. This would reduce the need for additional external funding.

Chapter 7

Task 7.1

Primary banks are those that are involved with the cheque clearing system.

True ☑

False ☐

Secondary banks are also known as commercial banks.

True ☐

False ☑

Task 7.2

The four main benefits of financial intermediation are:

- Small amounts deposited by savers can be combined to provide larger loan packages to businesses.
- Short-term savings can be transferred into long-term borrowings.
- Search costs are reduced as companies seeking loan finance can approach a bank directly rather than finding individuals to lend to them.
- Risk is reduced as an individual's savings are not tied up with one individual borrower directly.

Task 7.3

Bank ☑

Customer ☐

Task 7.4

A bank's main duties to its customers are:

- It must honour a customer's cheque provided that it is correctly made out, there is no legal reason for not honouring it and the customer has enough funds or overdraft limit to cover the amount of the cheque.

- The bank must credit cash/cheques that are paid into the customer's account.

- If the customer makes a written request for repayment of funds in their account, for example by writing a cheque, the bank must repay the amount on demand.

- The bank must comply with the customer's instructions given by direct debit mandate or standing order.

- The bank must provide a statement showing the transactions on the account within a reasonable period and provide details of the balance on the customer's account.

- The bank must respect the confidentiality of the customer's affairs unless the bank is required by law, public duty or its own interest to disclose details or where the customer gives their consent for such disclosure.

- The bank must tell the customer if there has been an attempt to forge the customer's signature on a cheque.

- The bank should use care and skill in its actions.

- The bank must provide reasonable notice if it is to close a customer's account.

Note: only six points were required.

Task 7.5

Use of money

You cannot restrict the ways in which the bank uses your money; the money can be used in any ways that are **legally and morally acceptable**. However, the bank must make the money available to you according to the terms of your deposit; if you are opening a current account it must be **available on demand**.

Overdrawn balances

If your account shows a negative or debit balance (an **overdraft**), the bank has the right to be repaid this balance on demand. The only exception is if the bank has granted you an **overdraft facility**, which requires the bank to give you a period of notice if it wishes you to pay back what you owe it.

Charges and commissions

The bank can charge you **interest** on overdrawn balances, and can also levy **other charges and commissions** for use of its services. Depending on the terms of your account, this can even include charges for drawing cheques from your account, and withdrawing money from cashpoint machines.

Duty of care

You owe the bank a duty of care, particularly when **drawing cheques**. You should not issue cheques that are signed but lack other details such as payee or amount, nor should you write cheques out in pencil as they can easily be altered.

You should also **take care of cards** that the bank issues to you (credit, debit and cashpoint cards) and keep your **PIN number** (the number that you need to enter to use the bank's cashpoint machines) secure.

Task 7.6

The most common reasons for a business identifying a future cash deficit or the need to raise additional finance are to:

• Fund day-to-day working capital
• Increase working capital
• Reduce payables
• Purchase non-current assets
• Acquire another business

Task 7.7

The correct answer is (i), (v), (vi)

Task 7.8

The correct answer is (ii), (iii), (iv)

Task 7.9

Type of finance	Advantages
Overdraft	Relatively low cost Precise amount required does not need to be known Security not normally required Covenants not normally included
Bank loan	Useful to fund capital expenditure Repayments can be negotiated

Task 7.10

Total interest cost (£)	£21,880
Simple annual interest rate %	11.4

Total repayments will be 36 × £2,380 = £85,680.

If the business has borrowed £63,800 to buy the tractor, the total interest cost is 85,680 − 63,800 = £21,880.

Over the three years of the loan, the total interest is 21,880/63,800 = 34.3%. This is equivalent to 11.4% simple interest per annum.

Task 7.11

Repayment of capital	£750
Repayment of interest	£98.44

Repayment of capital = 22,500/30 = £750 per month

Repayment of interest = (22,500 × 5.25%)/12 = £98.44

Task 7.12

Monthly interest rate (%)	0.33%

(Working: 4% × 1/12 = 0.33%)

Task 7.13

The APR on the loan would be   higher.

Flat rate interest is charged on   the original capital.

Task 7.14

(a)

	Arrangement fee £	Loan interest £	Overdraft interest £	Total cost £
Option 1	360	3,000		3,360
Option 2		2,400		2,400
Option 3	375	2,750	779	3,904

Note: overdraft interest is calculated as £8,500 × 11% × $^{10}/_{12}$ = £779

(b)

Option 1	✓
Option 2	
Option 3	
None of the options	

....

Task 7.15

(a) **Capital gearing**

Capital gearing is concerned with a company's **long-term capital structure**. The covenant attaching to the loan does not define clearly what is meant by capital gearing in this context, in particular whether the bank overdraft should be included as part of 'debt capital'. However, since it appears that the overdraft has been used principally to finance non-current assets in the form of machinery rather than as a source of working capital, it is probably reasonable to argue that it should be included as part of the prior charge capital. The gearing ratio can thus be defined as:

$$\frac{\text{Prior charge capital}}{\text{Shareholders' funds (equity)}} = \frac{\text{Debentures} + \text{overdraft}}{\text{Ordinary shares} + \text{reserves}}$$

The gearing ratio can now be calculated. $\dfrac{£5.0m + £3.0m}{£5.0 + £10.0m} = 53.3\%$

If the overdraft is ignored, the gearing ratio would be $\dfrac{£5.0m}{£5.0 + £10.0m} = 33.3\%$

(b) **Terms of covenant**

It appears from the calculation in part (a) that unless the overdraft is excluded, the company has already breached the covenant relating to the gearing level which states that 'At no time shall the ratio of debt capital to shareholders' funds exceed 50%'.

If short-term payables were included, the gearing would be increased.

The required liquidity range for the current ratio is 1.08 (1.35 × 80%) to 1.62 (1.35 × 120%). The current ratio (current assets: current liabilities) for Famous Ltd is 1.0 (£7.0m:£7.0m). The company is therefore in breach of the covenant with respect to liquidity.

(c) **Dangers of high gearing**

A **high gearing level** only constitutes a danger if the company is at risk of being unable to meet payments (including interest on the debt) as they fall due. If this situation arises the company could be forced to **liquidate assets** to meet the demands of its payables, and this in turn could jeopardise its operating viability. It follows that the absolute level of gearing cannot be used to assess the financial risk faced by the company. It is more helpful to assess the level of interest cover in the light of pattern of income and cash inflows. The company appears to have a stable business and pattern of income that allows it to meet its payables demands.

Quality of asset backing

A further factor to take into account is the **quality of the asset backing** since this will influence the attitude of its lenders if the company faces problems in repaying its debt. Land and buildings currently appear in the accounts at £9.0m, which represent 75% of the value of total payables (including trade payables). While it is unlikely that anything close to the book valuation of plant and machinery and inventory could be realised in the event of a forced sale, it is to be hoped that the major part of the receivables figures is collectable. Therefore, the company appears to have adequate asset backing in the event of a forced restructuring or liquidation.

Conclusion

The factors discussed above, when taken together, suggest that the **level of gearing** is not particularly dangerous. However, if the company is actually in breach of its loan covenants, the courses of action available to the lender and their attitude towards the situation will be of key importance in determining the true dangers of the company's position.

(d) **Lower Gearing**

Operating leases

If the company is to lower its capital gearing it needs either to increase the value of its issued share capital and reserves or to decrease the size of its borrowings. Since growth is low and cash resources relatively small it seems unlikely the company will be able to repay much of the debt in the short-term future from operational funds. However, one option might be to convert some of the owned plant and vehicles onto operating leases and thus reduce the size of the bank overdraft.

Sale and leaseback

Similarly the company might be able to raise funds through a sale and leaseback of property which could be used to reduce the level of debt. There may also be some scope to reduce the level of working capital through improving inventory and receivable turnovers and increasing the amount of credit taken from suppliers. However, the opportunities are likely to be limited: for example, the average debt collection period could probably not be reduced much below the current level of 52 days.

Increasing shareholders' funds

A rights issue could be used to increase the size of shareholders' funds include the following. The reaction of the market to a rights issue will depend on the rating of the company and the purpose for which the issue is being made.

Reduction in interest charges

Since the loan was taken out at a time when interest rates were very high, to reduce the level of its interest charges the company could take one of the following options:

Redeem the loan notes and replace with additional overdraft

This would reduce the interest cost by £5m × (15% − 9%) = £0.3m
The interest coverage would then become:
£3m ÷ (£1.0m − £0.3m) = 4.3 times

However the bank may be unlikely to agree to such a large increase in the overdraft facility given the purpose for which the finance is required.

Redeem the loan notes and replace with medium-term bond

This would reduce the interest cost by £5m × (15% − 5%) = £0.5m

The improvement in interest coverage makes this option, which has been put forward by the finance director, appear attractive.

Chapter 8

Task 8.1

The three main factors that should influence any decisions regarding investment of surplus funds are:

- Risk
- Return
- Liquidity

When cash is invested there are two main risks. There is the risk that the value of the investment will fall and there is also the risk that the return from the investment will be lower than expected due to changes in market interest rates. When a business is investing surplus funds it will generally wish to invest in investments where the risk of loss is fairly minimal.

The return on an investment has two potential aspects, the income return and the capital return. Most investments will pay some form of interest or dividend which is the income return. However, most investments will also tend to fluctuate in value over time and this is the capital return (or capital loss). In general, the higher the risk of an investment the higher will be the expected rate of return and *vice versa*.

Liquidity is the term used for the ease and speed with which an investment can be converted into cash. Any investments which are widely traded on a market, such as the money markets, will be very liquid but investments such as a bank deposit account which requires three months' notice to withdraw the funds would not be a liquid investment. The more liquid an investment is the lower the return is likely to be as less liquid investments will pay higher returns to attract investors.

Task 8.2

	Will accept ✓	Working
Investment paying interest of £300 every 6 months.		Total return = £600 (2 × £300) Rate of return = 600/20,000 = 3%
Investment with a lump sum return of £800 at the end of one year	✓	Rate of return = 800/20,000 = 4%
Investment paying annual interest of £600 plus a bonus of 1% of the capital invested if the deposit is retained for 1 year	✓	Total return = £600 + £200 bonus (1% × 20,000) = £800 Rate of return = 800/20,000 = 4%

The business is likely to be able to earn a higher rate of return if the period of time that the capital is available to invest increases.

True ✓

False

If the business wants to be able to withdraw funds on demand this is likely to increase the rate of return available.

True

False ✓

Task 8.3

The correct answer is: (iii), (iv), (v)

Task 8.4

Their price will rise. ✓

Their price will fall.

Task 8.5

	Bank deposit	Gilt-edged securities
Increase in value		
Decrease in value		✓
No effect	✓	

Task 8.6

Security procedures for the safe custody of cash include the following:

Physical procedures – any cash or cheques received must be kept safe at all times and must only be accessible to authorised individuals within the organisation. Therefore, cash should be kept under lock and key either in a cash box, lockable till or safe. Only authorised individuals should have access to the keys.

Checks for valid payment – payments received in cash will, of course, be valid provided that any notes are not forged. However if cheques are accepted as payment then they must be supported by a valid cheque guarantee card and be correctly drawn up, dated and signed. If debit or credit cards are accepted then basic checks should be made on the card and signature and authorisation must be sought for payments which exceed the floor limit.

Reconciliation of cash received – when payments are received in the form of cash, cheques or debit and credit cards then a list of all cash, cheque and card receipts taken during the day must be kept. This list must then be reconciled at the end of each day to the amount of cash in the till, cash box or safe. The list may be manual as each sale is made or may be automatically recorded on the till roll as each sale is rung in.

This reconciliation should not be carried out by the person responsible for making the sales but by some other responsible official. Any discrepancies between the amount of cash recorded as taken during the day and the amount physically left at the end of the day must be investigated.

Banking procedures – any cash, cheques and card vouchers should be banked as soon as possible and intact each day. This not only ensures the physical safety of the cash but also that it cannot be used by employees for unauthorised purposes. It also means that once the money is in the bank it is earning the business the maximum amount of interest. All cash should be banked as soon as possible but if it is not possible to bank it until the following day then either the cash must be left in a locked safe overnight or in the bank's overnight safe.

Recording procedures – for security purposes the paying-in slip for the bank should be made out by someone other than the person paying the money into the bank. The total on the paying-in slip should be reconciled to the till records or cash list for the day.

Task 8.7

Possible action	Strategy
Invest in marketable securities	(b)
Spend surplus cash	(c)
Repay surplus cash to owners	(a)
Retain cash for ease of availability	(d)

Justifications for answers

(a) No further growth/no plans for further capital expansion.

Action: An increased or **special dividend** should be paid to shareholders; the company could also consider a **share buyback**, by means of which shares would be repurchased from the shareholders and cancelled.

Reason: If no further investments are planned, cash surplus to the needs of the business should be **returned to shareholders** so that they can use it for other investment opportunities. A small cash surplus should however be maintained.

(b) Acquisition of manufacturer

Action: Invest the cash surplus in **marketable securities** (eg Certificates of Deposit, commercial paper) or bank deposits.

Reason: Such investments ensure that the company will make a **return on its money** while retaining sufficient liquidity for when it makes an acquisition.

(c) Development of new product lines

Action: **Spend** the **cash surplus** on the proposed capital investments.

Reason: Unless there is some other possible use for the funds, eg to fund an acquisition, it will be better to use the cash surplus rather than borrowing to **fund the capital investment**, since the cost of debt finance is likely to exceed the return achievable on cash investments.

(d) Acquisition of manufacturer and development of product lines

Action: **Retain the cash** until required for the acquisition. Fund the new product lines by borrowing or raising additional equity finance.

Reason: The cash will be **needed at short notice** for the acquisition. It should be easy to raise finance for the new product lines from external sources.

···

Task 8.8

(a)

	Investment of £50,000	Interest 2% above base rate	Convertible within 60 days	Low/medium risk	No shares
Option 1	✓		✓	✓	✓
Option 2	✓	✓		✓	✓
Option 3		✓	✓	✓	✓

(b)

Option 1	
Option 2	
Option 3	
None of the options	✓

(c) Attitudes to risk are generally categorised into three approaches.

Risk seeker

A risk seeker is a decision maker who is interested in the **best outcomes** no matter how **small** the **chance** that they may occur. They will choose the option which has the potential for the highest return, even if the risk is higher.

Risk averse

A risk averse decision maker acts on the assumption that the **worst outcome might occur**. If different investments offer the same return, they will choose the option with the least amount of risk involved. An alternative investment with higher risk would only be considered if it had a sufficiently higher expected return to compensate.

Risk neutral

A risk neutral decision maker prefers the most likely outcome. The decision can be made using probabilities to determine the expected value of the outcome – that is, based on what is **likely as a long-term average** and so no account is taken of whether the decision maker is risk averse or a risk seeker.

Given that the requirements of the company are that the investment is low or medium risk, the company can be said to be risk averse. The requirement to only invest in products that can be converted to cash within 60 days is another indication of an unwillingness to take risks.

···

Task 8.9

(a) Gilt-edged securities or gilts are ┌ marketable ┐ British Government securities.

They pay a ┌ fixed ┐ amount of interest and are available with varying

maturity dates which is the date ┌ on which they will be redeemed ┐.

(b) The correct answer is

Gilt-edged stocks	**Bank deposit account**
No change	Increase

Both a bank deposit account and gilts carry a stated rate of interest. However, they will be affected differently by changes in base interest rates.

With the bank deposit account if base rates change then the interest payable on the deposit will also normally change. However, the interest rate on the gilts will remain the same.

(c)   The correct answer is

Gilt-edged stocks	**Bank deposit account**
Decrease	No change

If interest rates increase the amount deposited in the bank account will not be affected and when the deposit matures the initial deposit will be the amount returned plus any accumulated interest.

However, gilts are marketable securities and as such their market value will fluctuate with changes in base rates. If the base rate of interest increases then the market value of any amount invested in gilts will fall. Whereas if market interest rates decrease the value of gilts will increase.

Task 8.10

The interest rate on the bank deposit account is 1.1% per quarter. This is equivalent to $(1.011_4 - 1) \times 100 = 4.47\%$ per annum.

The interest rate on the bond is 2.5% every six months. This is equivalent to $2.5\% \times 2 = 5\%$ per annum

Deposit account

Advantages

The deposit account is more flexible than the bonds which have a fixed date.

If market interest rates increase the return on the deposit account may also increase.

Disadvantages

The return offered is variable which means that if base rates fall, it may change.

In light of the global financial crisis and the failure of some banks, the deposit account would be considered more risky than government bonds.

Government Bond

Advantages

The main advantage is that a government bond is usually considered to be risk free. The interest rate per annum is also higher than the deposit account interest. This rate will be fixed.

Disadvantages

Bonds are not as flexible because they cannot be cashed in early. It is also possible that market interest rates will rise meaning that the return on the bond could be below market rate.

Task 8.11

Although an organisation may operate a finance function covering all its financial activities, there is a distinction between financial control activities and treasury activities.

Financial control activities involve the allocation and effective use of resources. This includes:

(i)   Analysing performance (management accounting)
(ii) Reporting results (financial accounting)
(iii) Advising on investment appraisal

Treasury activities involve managing liquidity, obtaining suitable types of finance and investing surplus funds. This includes:

(i)   Advising on sources of finance/potential investments
(ii) Financial risk management
(iii) Liaising with financial stakeholders (banks/financial intermediaries)

Large companies use the financial and currency markets heavily. These markets are volatile and changes can have a significant impact on a company's financial position. The advantage of having a separate treasury department, even if the team is small, is that they will be specialists in treasury management.

Treasury Department activities

If the Finance department identifies a financial issue such as a cash flow deficit the treasury function can advise on appropriate methods of raising finance and liaise with the sources of this finance to get the best deal for the company.

Whereas financial control functions may exist at a variety of local levels in a large organisation, the treasury department will be centralised at the head office and this brings economies of scale and specialism (e.g. they are able to negotiate better terms by pooling cash for investment or by amalgamating the funding requirements of individual business units).

The treasury department will also have the specialised skills required to assess performance in cash management with reference to the risk, return and liquidity needs of the organisation.

Task 8.12

To: Director of SelfBuild Ltd
From: Assistant Accountant
Re: Investment of cash surplus

In the case of this cash surplus the issues are as follows:

1.   This cash is needed to **pay for the factory**. Therefore the risk of loss must be minimised, even at the cost of lower returns during the period of investment.

2.   The cash will be needed in **3 – 4 months**. Therefore it cannot be tied up for a longer period.

I have looked at the three possible investment opportunities and found the following in relation to risk and return:

(i) **Treasury bills.** These are virtually risk free

Purchased now and held for 91 days, they will give us a return of 1% (1000 – 990/990) over the three months.

This equates to a simple annual yield of 4% (1% over 3 months × 4).

(ii) **Equities** are higher yield (10%) but with a far higher level of risk. We have no way of knowing how the share index will perform over three months and we may end up selling at a loss in order to release the cash. If the shares are sold before the dividend is declared we will lose the dividend.

(iii) **A bank deposit account** will pay 3.5% per annum. This is slightly less than Treasury bills but is also virtually risk-free and only requires 30 days notice. If notice is not given, a month's interest will be lost.

The best option would appear to be the Treasury bills for 91 days. If at the end of that time the cash is not needed for another month it could be put into a bank deposit account.

AAT AQ2013 SAMPLE ASSESSMENT 1
CASH MANAGEMENT

Time allowed: 2.5 hours

AAT AQ2013
SAMPLE ASSESSMENT

Task 1 (12 marks)

The following forecast information has been provided for a company for the next year, 20X4.

Forecast Statement of Profit or Loss for the year ended 31 December 20X4	£	£
Sales revenue		500,000
Less: Cost of sales		
Opening inventory	70,000	
Purchases	300,000	
Closing inventory	(70,000)	
Cost of sales		300,000
Gross profit		200,000
Expenses		120,000
Operating profit		80,000
Tax		21,000
Profit after tax		59,000

Additional information

1. The company believes that 90% of sales will be on credit terms. 10% of total sales will be cash sales. The balance of trade receivables at 1 January 20X4 is forecast to be £90,000 and the company expects trade receivables at 31 December 20X4 to be equivalent to 20% of the total sales for the year.

2. All purchases are to be made on credit terms. The balance of trade payables at 1 January 20X4 is forecast to be £45,000. Total payments for purchases during the year have been forecast as £295,000.

3. Expenses include a depreciation charge of £20,000 with all other expenses being settled on cash terms.

4. The carrying value of non-current assets at 1 January 20X4 is forecast to be £320,000 and the carrying value of non-current assets at 31 December 20X4 is forecast to be £375,000. The company will pay for any additions immediately by cash.

5. The tax payable shown on the Statement of Financial Position is expected to be £20,000 at 1 January 20X4 and £22,000 at 31 December 20X4.

6. The forecast cash position at 1 January 20X4 is £28,000 in hand.

Use the table below to forecast the closing cash position at 31 December 20X4.

Use brackets or minus signs where appropriate.

	£
Operating profit	80,000
Change in trade receivables	
Change in trade payables	
Adjustment for non-cash items	
Purchase of non-current assets	
Tax paid	
Net change in cash position	
Forecast cash position 1 January 20X4	28,000
Forecast cash position 31 December 20X4	

Task 2 (14 marks)

The price of a commodity is set on the first day of every month. The price for the last four months is given in the table below.

(a) **Create an index for the price of the commodity using month 1 as the base period.**

Month	1	2	3	4
Price	£168.00	£181.44	£189.84	£204.96
Index				

A company uses the least squares regression line to forecast sales. The regression line has been identified as:

y = 316,000 + 1,800x

where y is the sales value and x is the period. September 20X4 was period 22.

(b) **Complete the following sentence.**

The forecast value of sales for December 20X4 using the regression line is:

£

(c) **Assuming that each unit has a selling price of £25, the forecast sales volume for December 20X4 based on the calculation in part (b) is** [   ] **units.**

The cost of manufacturing product PD81 is £190.

(d) **Calculate the forecast selling price of the product if the company requires a mark up of 40% or a margin of 20%.**

The forecast selling price to achieve a mark up of 40% is:

£ [   ] (to the nearest penny).

The forecast selling price to achieve a margin of 20% is:

£ [   ] (to the nearest penny).

Task 3 (14 marks)

A company has supplied information regarding its forecast sales, labour costs and purchases.

Sales

Sales volume has been forecast for periods 1 to 5. Each product sells for £30.

The company estimates that 15% of sales are made on a cash basis with the balance made on a credit basis.

An analysis of historical data shows that credit customers settle their debts on the basis of 30% one month after the date of sale and 70% two months after the date of sale.

	Period 1	Period 2	Period 3	Period 4	Period 5
Sales volume (units)	8,200	8,500	8,800	6,100	5,400

(a) **Complete the table below to identify the total sales receipts forecast for periods 4 and 5. Identify the forecast trade receivables balance at the end of period 5.**

	Period 4 £	Period 5 £
Total sales receipts		

The trade receivables balance at the end of period 5 is forecast to be:

£ [   ]

Labour costs

Labour costs include hourly paid employees and four-weekly paid employees. The labour costs for hourly paid employees are calculated based on the number of hours worked multiplied by a standard hourly rate of £11. Hourly paid employees are paid overtime at an overtime rate of £14 per hour. The company also employs two supervisors who are each paid an annual salary of £26,000. The year is divided into 13 four-week periods.

Hourly paid employees are paid their standard hours in the period incurred and overtime hours in the following period. The supervisors are paid on the last day of each period.

The forecast standard and overtime hours are given below.

	Period 1	Period 2	Period 3	Period 4	Period 5
Forecast standard hours worked	1,400	1,560	1,620	1,320	1,300
Forecast overtime hours worked	250	318	140	60	25

(b) **Complete the table below to identify the total payments for labour costs forecast for periods 4 and 5.**

	Period 4 £	Period 5 £
Total labour costs		

Purchases

The company pays its suppliers on the basis of 25% one month after the date of purchase, 40% two months after the date of purchase and 35% three months after the date of purchase.

At the end of period 3 the balance of trade payables is forecast to be:

	£
Balance from Period 1	30,135
Balance from Period 2	66,900
Balance from Period 3	92,400
Trade payables at the end of period 3	189,435

(c) **Complete the table below to identify the value of trade payables at the end of period 3 that will be paid in periods 4 and 5.**

	Period 4 £	Period 5 £
Settlement of trade payables		

Task 4 (16 marks)

The cash budget for a company has been partially completed for two periods. The following information is to be incorporated and the cash budget completed.

- The company has £520,000 invested in a fixed term, fixed interest investment. Interest is earned at 0.4% per period and is credited to the bank on the first day of each period.

- The company plans to issue 225,000 ordinary shares of £1 each in period 6 at an issue price of £1.30 per share.

- The business has contracted to purchase plant and machinery for £178,000. The supplier has agreed that the company can pay a deposit of £50,000 in period 2 with 70% of the balance payable in period 5 and the remaining balance payable in period 6.

- Overdraft interest is payable at 0.4% per period based on the previous period's closing overdraft balance.

- The company took out a bank loan in period 3 of £162,000. The loan term is 20 periods beginning in period 4. Interest of 5% is added at the beginning of the loan term and the monthly repayments include both capital and interest elements.

- The company has to pay tax of £242,000 in period 6.

- The balance on the business bank account is expected to be overdrawn by £120,000 at the end of period 4.

Using the additional information above, complete the cash budget for the company for periods 5 and 6.

Cash inflows should be entered as positive figures and cash outflows as negative figures (use brackets or minus signs).

Round to the nearest whole £ throughout.

Cash Budget	Period 5 £	Period 6 £
RECEIPTS		
Receipts from sales	336,200	360,000
Proceeds from share issue		
Investment income		
Total receipts		
PAYMENTS		
Purchases	(62,400)	(68,000)
Wages	(112,000)	(120,000)
Other operating expenses	(19,295)	(20,600)
Purchase of plant and machinery		
Tax payment		
Bank overdraft interest		
Bank loan repayment		
Total payments		
Net cash flow		
Opening bank balance		
Closing bank balance		

Task 5 (16 marks)

A company is setting up a new division to manufacture and sell product PD22X. The product is seasonal and the sales have been forecast as follows:

	Period 1 £	Period 2 £	Period 3 £	Period 4 £	Period 5 £	Period 6 £	Total £
Forecast sales	492,000	516,000	530,000	450,000	420,000	380,000	2,788,000

Based on the sales of other products the company estimated that 10% of sales would be paid in the period of sale; 30% of sales would be paid in the period after sale; 45% of sales would be paid two periods after sale and 15% of sales would be paid three periods after sale. The expected sales receipts on this basis have already been calculated for periods 1 to 4 and are shown in the table below.

	Period 1 £	Period 2 £	Period 3 £	Period 4 £	Total £
Original forecast sales receipts	49,200	199,200	429,200	510,000	1,187,600

The company is now considering offering a 10% settlement discount for all credit sales settled in the period after sale. It is now expected that 10% of sales would be paid in the the period of sale, 55% of sales would be paid in the period after sale, 25% of sales would be paid two periods after sale and 10% of sales would be paid three periods after sale.

(a) **Complete the table below to calculate the sales receipts expected in periods 1 to 4 if the settlement discount is offered.**

	Forecast sales £	Sales receipts				
		Period 1 £	Period 2 £	Period 3 £	Period 4 £	Total £
Period 1 sales	492,000	49,200				
Period 2 sales	516,000		51,600			
Period 3 sales	530,000			53,000		
Period 4 sales	450,000				45,000	
Revised forecast sales receipts		49,200				

(b) **Complete the sentences below.**

Receipts from sales in periods 1 to 4 will [▼] by [ ] % if the settlement discount is offered. The settlement discount will [▼] total profit by: £ [ ] which is equivalent to [ ] % of total sales.

Drop-down list:

Decrease
Increase
Increase
Reduce

(c) **Which one of the following identifies the impact on cash flow of offering a settlement discount to credit customers?**

Total cash receipts remain the same but customers take less time to pay. ☐

Total cash receipts reduce but customers take less time to pay. ☐

Total cash receipts increase but customers take less time to pay. ☐

Total cash receipts remain the same but customers take longer to pay. ☐

Total cash receipts reduce and customers take longer to pay. ☐

Total cash receipts increase but customers take longer to pay. ☐

Task 6 (12 marks)

The budgeted and actual cash flows for an organisation are summarised in the table below. A variance which is 5% or more of the original budget is deemed to be significant and needs to be investigated.

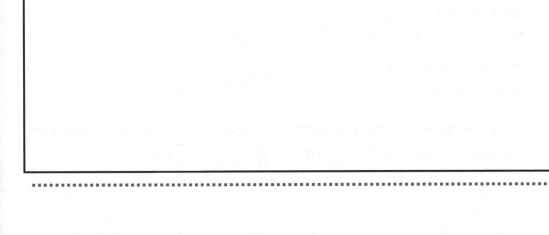

	Budgeted	Actual £	Variance £	A/F
RECEIPTS				
Cash sales	27,000	25,380	1,620	A
Credit sales	124,600	133,325	8,725	F
Total receipts	151,600	158,705		
PAYMENTS				
Cash purchases	5,300	5,538	238	A
Credit purchases	48,000	49,880	1,880	A
Wages and salaries	32,800	31,144	1,656	F
General expenses	15,400	14,800	600	F
Capital expenditure	20,000	21,000	1,000	A
Total payments	121,500	122,362		
Net cash flow	30,100	36,343		

Identify each of the significant variances for the period. Provide possible reasons why the variance might have occurred, suggest corrective actions where appropriate and identify implications for future budget setting.

Task 7 (12 marks)

(a) **Monetary policy is a process where a central bank**

Increases or decreases the supply of certificates of deposits.

Increases or decreases the supply of money.

Increases or decreases the value of loans to businesses.

Increases or decreases rates of tax on individuals and businesses.

(b) **In times of recession banks often**

Increase the availability of loans and overdrafts.

Convert overdrafts to loans to obtain a fixed charge.

Convert loans to overdrafts to increase interest earned.

Restrict the availability of loans and overdrafts.

The following figures have been extracted from the financial statements of a company for the year ended 31 December 20X4.

Statement of Financial Position (Extract) for the year ended	31 December 20X4 £
Inventories	110,502
Trade receivables	157,860
Trade payables	76,958

Statement of Profit or Loss (Extract) for the year ended	31 December 20X4 £
Sales	1,200,400
Cost of sales	720,240

(c) **Calculate the following:**

The inventory holding period is [   ] days.

The trade receivables collection period is [   ] days.

The trade payables payment period is [   ] days.

(d) **Using answers from part (c) calculate the cash operating cycle for the company.**

The cash operating cycle for the company is [   ] days.

Task 8 (12 marks)

(a) **Which of the following best describes a variable rate of interest?**

Interest rate that is guaranteed not to exceed a specified level. ☐

Interest rate that remains the same for the period of borrowing. ☐

Interest charge that floats in line with bank base rates. ☐

Interest rate that fluctuates in line with an agreed indicator. ☐

(b) **What term is used to describe the effective rate of interest that a borrower will pay on a loan?**

Annual Percentage Rate ☐

Average Percentage Rate ☐

Actual Percentage Rate ☐

Actual Perfect Rate ☐

(c) **How much will an investor need to invest for one year to earn £3,080 interest, assuming a fixed annual rate of interest of 2.8%?**

£ [＿＿＿＿＿＿] will need to be invested to earn annual interest of £3,080 at a fixed interest rate of 2.8%.

(d) **A bank has offered to lend a company £80,000 to be repaid in 12 monthly instalments of £6,900 per month.**

The flat rate of interest being charged is [＿＿＿＿＿＿] %.

(e) **Calculate the interest yield (to 2 decimal places) on 6.4% Treasury Stock 20X4 with a current market price of £116.**

The interest yield is [＿＿＿＿＿＿] %.

(f) **Which of the following are types of security for borrowing?**

(i) Floating charge

(ii) Fixed charge

(iii) Variable charge

(iv) Loan charge

(i) and (ii) only ☐

(iii) and (iv) only ☐

(i), (ii) and (iii) only ☐

(ii), (iii) and (iv) only ☐

All of them ☐

Task 9 (16 marks)

A company needs to acquire some new plant and is considering the most appropriate means of funding the purchase. The purchase price of the plant is £250,000.

Three options are being considered:

1. Hire purchase agreement for 4 years.
2. Operating lease with a minimum term of 5 years.
3. Issue of equity shares to cover the cost of the purchase.

Prepare notes for the directors of the company which identify the main features of each of the financing options and sets out the implications of each option on the financial position of the company as shown on the Statement of Profit or Loss and the Statement of Financial Position. You should comment specifically on how the gearing of the company will be affected by each option.

Notes for the Directors on various financing options

1. **Hire purchase agreement for 4 years.**

2. **Operating lease with a minimum term of 5 years.**

3.   Issue of equity shares to cover the cost of purchase.

Task 10 (12 marks)

A company has £500,000 surplus cash and the treasurer estimates that the cash is free to be invested for up to three years.

Write a report to the finance director of the company which considers the risk, return and liquidity of each of the following investment options:

*   **Land**
*   **Long term bank deposit account**
*   **Shares in public companies**

Report to the Finance Director considering the risk, return and liquidity of investing in land, a long term bank deposit account and shares in public companies.

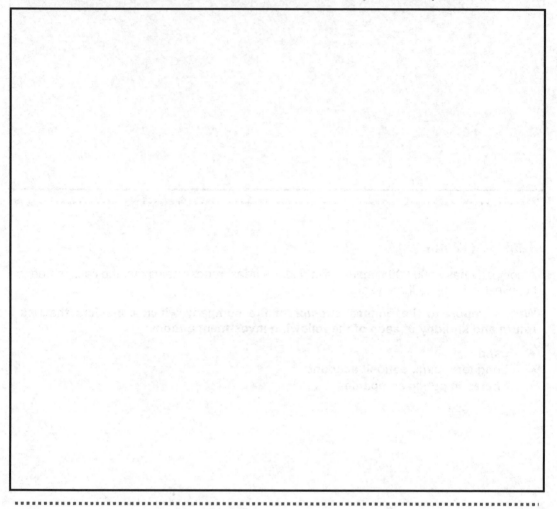

AAT AQ2013 SAMPLE ASSESSMENT 1
CASH MANAGEMENT

ANSWERS

Task 1 (12 marks)

	£
Operating profit	80,000
Change in trade receivables	−10,000
Change in trade payables	5,000
Adjustment for non-cash items	20,000
Purchase of non-current assets	−75,000
Tax paid	−19,000
Net change in cash position	1,000
Forecast cash position 1 January 20X4	28,000
Forecast cash position 31 December 20X4	29,000

Task 2 (14 marks)

(a)

Month	1	2	3	4
Price	£168.00	£181.44	£189.84	£204.96
Index		108	113	122

(b) The forecast value of sales for December 20X4 using the regression line is:

£ | 361,000 |

(c) | 14,440 | **units.**

(d) The forecast selling price to achieve a mark up of 40% is:

£ | 266.00 | (to the nearest penny).

The forecast selling price to achieve a margin of 20% is:

£ | 237.50 | (to the nearest penny).

Task 3 (14 marks)

(a)

	Period 4 £	Period 5 £
Total sales receipts	246,495	228,045

The trade receivables balance at the end of period 5 is forecast to be:

£ 246,585

(b)

	Period 4 £	Period 5 £
Total labour costs	20,480	19,140

(c)

	Period 4 £	Period 5 £
Settlement of trade payables	88,915	68,180

Task 4 (16 marks)

Cash Budget	Period 5 £	Period 6 £
RECEIPTS		
Receipts from sales	336,200	360,000
Proceeds from share issue	0	292,500
Investment income	2,080	2,080
Total receipts	338,280	654,580
PAYMENTS		
Purchases	(62,400)	(68,000)
Wages	(112,000)	(120,000)
Other operating expenses	(19,295)	(20,600)
Purchase of plant and machinery	−89,600	−38,400
Tax payment	0	242,000
Bank overdraft interest	−480	−296
Bank loan repayment	−8,505	−8,505
Total payments	−292,280	−497,801
Net cash flow	46,000	156,779
Opening bank balance	−120,000	−74,000
Closing bank balance	−74,000	82,779

Task 5 (16 marks)

(a) **Complete the table below to calculate the sales receipts expected in periods 1 to 4 if the settlement discount is offered.**

	Forecast sales £	Sales receipts				
		Period 1 £	Period 2 £	Period 3 £	Period 4 £	Total £
Period 1 sales	492,000	49,200	243,540	123,000	49,200	
Period 2 sales	516,000		51,600	255,420	129,000	
Period 3 sales	530,000			53,000	262,350	
Period 4 sales	450,000				45,000	
Revised forecast sales receipts		49,200	295,140	431,420	485,550	1,261,310

(b) **Complete the sentences below.**

Receipts from sales in periods 1 to 4 will [increase ▼] by [6.21] % if the settlement discount is offered. The settlement discount will [reduce ▼] total profit by: £ [153,340] which is equivalent to [5.5] % of total sales.

(c) **Which one of the following identifies the impact on cash flow of offering a settlement discount to credit customers?**

Total cash receipts remain the same but customers take less time to pay. ☐

Total cash receipts reduce but customers take less time to pay. ☑

Total cash receipts increase but customers take less time to pay. ☐

Total cash receipts remain the same but customers take longer to pay. ☐

Total cash receipts reduce and customers take longer to pay. ☐

Total cash receipts increase but customers take longer to pay. ☐

Task 6 (12 marks)

Cash sales (6% adverse)

Possible reasons

- More customers taking advantage of credit terms
- There could have been a decrease in sales volume or a reduction in selling price
- Inaccurate forecasting
- Depending on the product sales could have been affected by economic or environmental factors

Possible actions

- If sales volumes have deceased then improvements may need to be made to the product
- Better marketing strategies to improve sales volume
- If prices have been permanently discounted then revise future budgets accordingly

Credit sales (7% favourable)

Possible reasons

- Increased credit sales leading to increased receipts
- Improved credit control procedures

Possible actions

- If sales volumes have not improved then it is possible that the favourable variance in this period will result in an adverse variance in subsequent periods and therefore future budgets should take this into consideration

Wages and salaries (5.05% favourable)

Possible reasons

- If sales volumes are falling then direct wages may fall if manufacturing is reduced
- Less overtime may have been needed during the period
- There may have been a reduction in staff due to natural wastage or leavers which have reduced the payroll costs for the period

Possible actions

- If there has been a reduction in manufacturing or staff levels and this is expected to continue then future budgets will need to be adjusted accordingly
- If production levels have remained constant and have been accomplished without the need for overtime then identify any changes in production processes that have enabled this and continue for the future
- If the reduction is due to staff leaving which will need to be replaced then future budgets should not be reduced

<u>Capital expenditure (5% adverse)</u>

Possible reasons

- Earlier expenditure may have been deferred to this period
- Prices may have increased since the budget was set
- The supplier may have reduced the availability of credit for capital purchases
- More assets or higher specification assets may have been purchased

Possible actions

- Future capital expenditure could be contracted for in advance with prices and payment terms agreed to avoid unexpected increases
- Capital expenditure could be deferred to a later period to avoid an adverse variance

Task 7 (12 marks)

(a) **Monetary policy is a process where a central bank**

Increases or decreases the supply of certificates of deposits. ☐

Increases or decreases the supply of money. ✓

Increases or decreases the value of loans to businesses. ☐

Increases or decreases rates of tax on individuals and businesses. ☐

(b) **In times of recession banks often**

Increase the availability of loans and overdrafts. ☐

Convert overdrafts to loans to obtain a fixed charge. ☐

Convert loans to overdrafts to increase interest earned. ☐

Restrict the availability of loans and overdrafts. ✓

(c) **Calculate the following:**

The inventory holding period is | 56 | days.

The trade receivables collection period is | 48 | days.

The trade payables payment period is | 39 | days.

(d) **Using answers from part (c) calculate the cash operating cycle for the company.**

The cash operating cycle for the company is | 65 | days.

Task 8 (12 marks)

(a) **Which of the following best describes a variable rate of interest?**

Interest rate that is guaranteed not to exceed a specified level. ☐

Interest rate that remains the same for the period of borrowing. ☐

Interest charge that floats in line with bank base rates. ☐

Interest rate that fluctuates in line with an agreed indicator. ☑

(b) **What term is used to describe the effective rate of interest that a borrower will pay on a loan?**

Annual Percentage Rate ☑

Average Percentage Rate ☐

Actual Percentage Rate ☐

Actual Perfect Rate ☐

(c) **How much will an investor need to invest for one year to earn £3,080 interest, assuming a fixed annual rate of interest of 2.8%?**

£ | 110,000 | will need to be invested to earn annual interest of £3,080 at a fixed interest rate of 2.8%.

(d) **A bank has offered a lend a company £80,000 to be repaid in 12 monthly instalments of £6,900 per month.**

The flat rate of interest being charged is | 3.5 | %.

(e) **Calculate the interest yield (to 2 decimal places) on 6.4% Treasury Stock 20X4 with a current market price of £116.**

The interest yield is | 5.52 | %.

(f) **Which of the following are types of security for borrowing?**

(i) Floating charge

(ii) Fixed charge

(iii) Variable charge

(iv) Loan charge

(i) and (ii) only	✓
(iii) and (iv) only	☐
(i), (ii) and (iii) only	☐
(ii), (iii) and (iv) only	☐
All of them	☐

Task 9 (16 marks)

Hire purchase agreement

- A hire purchase agreement will enable the company to purchase the plant and pay for it in instalments over 4 years

- Interest will be charged based on the balance outstanding and an interest rate set at the beginning of the finance term

- The plant will remain the property of the hire purchase company until all the instalments have been made however the company will be responsible for repairs and maintenance during the term of the hire purchase agreement

- As the company will have substantially all of the risks and rewards of ownership the plant will be shown on the statement of financial position as an asset at its full purchase price

- The balance of the hire purchase outstanding will be shown as a liability on the statement of financial position. The amount due within one year will be included with current liabilities and the balance with non-current liabilities

- Interest paid on the loan will be debited to the statement of profit or loss

- The balance of the loan in non-current liabilities is classed as long term debt and will therefore be included in the gearing calculation

- The gearing of the company will increase which could affect the company's ability to raise additional finance. The plant will not be available for other lenders to take as security because the hire purchase company will hold title until the final repayment has been made

Operating lease

- This is a straight forward lease agreement where the company would hire the plant

- The leasing company would retain ownership of the assets however some operating lease agreements require the lessee to maintain and repair the asset

- The lease payments are included in the statement of profit or loss

- The asset is not included on the statement of financial position and the obligation under the operating lease is not included in liabilities

- The obligation under the operating lease will be included as a note in the financial statements but will not be included in the calculation of gearing

- The company will show reduced profits due to the lease repayments

Equity injection

- The company will raise funds from the existing shareholders of the business, from new shareholders or from a combination of both

- The additional funds raised will be used to purchase the plant outright

- The plant will be included in non-current assets on the statement of financial position

- There will not be any cost to the statement of profit or loss because there will be no borrowing associated with the asset and therefore no interest payments to be made

- The equity position on the statement of financial position will increase which will have the effect of reducing gearing assuming that there is no other increase in long term borrowings

- The company will be in a stronger position to raise additional finance with lower gearing and the plant available as security

- If the shares are offered to new investors then existing shareholders will experience a dilution of control and possibly earnings which may cause discontent

Task 10 (12 marks)

Land

- Historically land is deemed to be a fairly safe investment as there is a finite supply

- However in the last decade land values have been volatile sometimes resulting in a capital loss for investors

- Therefore the initial investment of £500,000 may not be fully realised if the market value is lower than £500,000 at the date of sale

- Land is usually seen as a long term investment and may take longer than three years to make a suitable return for the company

- The investment can only be realised once the land is sold and the speed of this will depend upon the economic environment at the time of sale

- The liquidity of the company may be adversely affected if they are unable to realise the full £500,000 at the end of three years

- It is unlikely that the return could be forecast with any certainty at the time of purchase

Long term bank deposit account

- Investment in a bank deposit account is generally perceived to be a low risk option

- The return is likely to reflect the low risk and therefore be substantially less than could be earned on other investments

- Traditionally bank deposit accounts were seen as risk free from the perspective of the loss of capital value. However in light of the global financial crisis there is a risk of loss of capital value if the deposit is not covered by a government backed guarantee scheme

- The deposit account may have a minimum notice period to avoid early withdrawal however the funds could be available immediately if required even though the company would achieve a lower return than expected

Shares in public companies

- Shares in public companies are generally perceived to be high risk because of market volatility and lack of control over business decisions made by those running the company

- However high returns can be achieved with the right portfolio of shares held for a reasonable period of time

- The company could spread the risk by selecting a portfolio which includes both low risk and high risk companies

- The return achievable cannot be identified with any certainty at the time of investment

- As shares can be sold at any point after purchase it would take only a few days for the company to realise its cash as long as it is prepared to take the price offered at that point in time

- The company could also realise its cash piecemeal as and when required

- The fees for buying and selling will need to be offset against any dividends and increase in share price when calculating the return

AAT AQ2013 SAMPLE ASSESSMENT 2
CASH MANAGEMENT

Time allowed: 2.5 hours

Cash Management (CSHM)

Introduction

We have provided the following assessment to help you familiarise yourself with AAT's e-assessment environment. It is designed to demonstrate as many as possible of the question types you may find in a live assessment. It is not designed to be used on its own to determine whether you are ready for a live assessment.

Each task is independent. You will not need to refer to your answers to previous tasks. Read every task carefully to make sure you understand what is required.

Where the date is relevant, it is given in the task data.
Both minus signs and brackets can be used to indicate negative numbers UNLESS task instructions say otherwise.

You must use a full stop to indicate a decimal point. For example, write 100.57 NOT 100,57 or 100 57.

You may use a comma to indicate a number in the thousands, but you don't have to. For example, 10000 and 10,000 are both OK.

Other indicators are not compatible with the computer-marked system.

Complete all 10 tasks.

Task 1 (12 marks)

The following forecast information has been provided for a company for the year 20X3, and the forecast for the year 20X4.

Extracts from the Statement of Financial Position as at 31 December	Actual 20X3	Forecast 20X4
	£	£
Non-current assets	480,000	800,000
Current assets		
Inventory	230,000	357,000
Receivables	256,000	288,000
Cash	212,000	0
Current liabilities		
Bank overdraft	0	54,000
Trade payables	63,000	99,000
Taxation payable	55,000	66,000
Net assets	1,060,000	1,226,000

Additional information

1. The sales forecast for 20X4 is £780,000.

2. The company is not forecasting to sell any non-current assets during the year. There are forecast additions which have been included in the movement on non-current assets in the extract from the Statement of Financial Position.

3. Expenses include a depreciation charge of £62,000 with all other expenses being settled on cash terms.

4. Actual operating profit for the year 20X3 was £185,000 and the forecast operating profit for the year 20X4 is £232,000.

5. The forecast tax charge for 20X4 is £66,000.

Use the table below to reconcile the opening cash position with the forecast closing cash position at 31 December 20X4. Use minus signs where appropriate.

	£
Operating profit	
Change in inventories	
Change in trade receivables	
Change in trade payables	
Adjustment for non-cash items	
Purchase of non-current assets	
Tax paid	_____
Net change in cash position	
Forecast cash position 1 January 20X4	_____
Forecast cash position 31 December 20X4	_____

Task 2 (14 marks)

A company is preparing its forecast sales for next year. The sales volume trend is to be identified using a 3-point moving average based on the actual sales volumes for the current year.

(a) **Complete the table below, calculate the monthly sales volume trend and identify any monthly variations. Enter minus signs where appropriate, and round to the nearest whole number.**

Period	Sales volume (units)	Trend	Monthly variation (Volume less trend)
1	1,817		
2	1,650		
3	1,648		
4	2,120		
5	2,085		
6	1,741		
7	1,700		
8	2,214		

(b) **Calculate the average monthly trend.** _____

....

A colleague has calculated that sales in period 13 will be 2,065 units, and that the monthly trend has changed to 35 units.

(c) **Assuming there is no monthly variation in months 15 and 16, calculate the forecast sales and complete the table below.**

Month 15 (units)	Month 16 (units)

....

The selling price per unit is based on cost plus 40%.

The purchase price per unit in period 5 was £435 when the cost index was 145.

The cost index for period 16 is expected to be 180.

(d) **Calculate the selling price for period 16.**

£ ☐

....

Task 3 (14 marks)

A company has supplied the following information for the coming periods for a new division.

	Period 1	Period 2	Period 3	Period 4	Period 5	Period 6
Sales volume (units)	12,400	12,600	12,200	11,800	12,800	13,500
	£	£	£	£	£	£
Sales price per unit	12	12	12	12	12	12
Sales revenue	148,800	151,200	146,400	141,600	153,600	162,000
Opening inventory	65,000	68,900	70,850	73,450	81,250	75,400
Purchases	84,500	83,850	81,900	84,500	77,350	78,000
Closing inventory	(68,900)	(70,850)	(73,450)	(81,250)	(75,400)	(65,650)
Cost of sales	80,600	81,900	79,300	76,700	83,200	87,750
Gross profit	68,200	69,300	67,100	64,900	70,400	74,250

Sales

The company estimates that 15% of sales are paid in the month that the sale is made, 35% are paid in the following month, while 45% are paid in two months. The balance is potential irrecoverable debt and a provision for irrecoverable debt is charged in the month of sale.

(a) **Complete the table below to identify the total sales receipts forecast for periods 5 and 6. Identify the forecast trade receivables balance at the end of period 3 and the irrecoverable debt provision for period 4.**

	Period 5 £	Period 6 £
Total sales receipts		

The trade receivables balance at the end of period 3 is forecast to be:

£ _____

The provision for irrecoverable debts for period 4 is forecast to be:

£ _____

....

Purchases

The company pays its suppliers on the basis of 45% one month after the date of purchase and 55% two months after the date of purchase.

(b) **At the end of period 3 the balance of trade payables is forecast to be:**

£ _____

....

(c) **Complete the table below to identify the value of trade payables that will be paid in periods 4 and 5.**

	Period 4 £	Period 5 £
Settlement of trade payables		

....

Task 4 (16 marks)

Wilson Plc has provided the following partially completed cash budget for period 6 and period 7. Further information has been provided to determine the cash inflows and outflows to and from the company.

- The company issued 1.3 million ordinary shares with a £1 nominal value. The current market value of each share is £1.37 and these shares were issued at a purchase price of £1.30. The company will receive this income in period 6.

- The company will invest £1.3 million in a fixed rate account paying interest at 2.8% above base rate and will receive this monthly income for the first time in period 7. The current base rate of interest is 0.5%.

- The company sold a non-current asset in period 6 and made of a loss of £7,830. The asset originally cost £84,000 and 75% of the asset had been depreciated.

- To replace the above asset the company purchased a replacement in period 6 for £116,000 and paid a 40% deposit in this period. The remaining balance will be paid in 8 equal instalments commencing in period 7.

- The company has within the last few months taken a mortgage out on their premises. The premises cost £4,000,000 and the mortgage was 90% loan to value. The mortgage is over a 10 year period and interest is charged on the initial balance at 4% per annum on a flat rate of interest basis. Payments are made on a monthly basis and include both interest and capital.

- Prior to the issue of additional shares a dividend was declared for the 4,000,000 shares already in issue and will pay the dividend in period 7 at 12p per share.

- Wilson prepared its VAT return for the quarter ending period 5. The sales for the quarter were £2,200,000 net with purchases of £1,480,000 net. The VAT rate is 20% and any VAT payment or refund will be made or received in period 6.

- The company has an investment portfolio of properties which cost £280,000. The rental yield is 6% and the rent is received monthly.

- The overdrawn bank balance at the end of period 5 was £840,000. Overdraft interest is charged at 12% per annum, is calculated on the balance at the end of the period and paid in the following period.

Using additional information above, complete the cash budget for the company for periods 6 and 7. Cash inflows should be entered as positive figures and cash outflows as negative figures (use brackets or minus signs). Round to the nearest whole £ throughout.

Cash Budget	Period 6 £	Period 7 £
RECEIPTS		
Sales receipts	2,403,332	2,198,462
Share issue		
Investment income		
Rental income		
Sale of non-current asset	_____	_____
Total receipts	══════	══════
PAYMENTS		
Purchases	(1,432,096)	(950,132)
Wages and salaries	(526,636)	(492,713)
General expenses	(32,000)	(30,000)
Mortgage payment		
VAT payment to HMRC		
Purchase of non-current assets		
Dividend payment		
Overdraft interest	_____	_____
Total payments	══════	══════
Net cash flow		
Opening bank balance		
Closing bank balance		

Task 5 (16 marks)

A company is setting up a new division to sell product PDQ. The sales have been forecast as follows:

	Period 1	Period 2	Period 3	Period 4	Total
Forecast sales volume (units)	12,500	13,500	13,700	14,200	53,900
Forecast sales price	£200	£200	£200	£200	£200
Forecast sales revenue	£2,500,000	£2,700,000	£2,740,000	£2,840,000	£10,780,000

Based on the sales of other products the company estimated that 42% of sales would be paid in the period after sale, 38% of sales would be paid two periods after sale and 20% of sales would be paid three periods after sale. The expected sales receipts on this basis have already been calculated for periods 1 to 4 and are shown in the table below.

	Period 1 £	Period 2 £	Period 3 £	Period 4 £	Total £
Original forecast sales receipts	0	1,050,000	2,084,000	2,676,800	5,810,800

The company is now considering offering extended credit terms to encourage sales. The revised credit terms are expected to increase sales volumes by 10%. 60% of the revised estimated sales are now expected to be received two periods after sale, and 40% of sales three periods after sale.

(a) **Complete the table below to calculate the forecast sales receipts expected in periods 1 to 4 if the revised credit terms are offered.**

	Period 1 £	Period 2 £	Period 3 £	Period 4 £
Forecast sales receipts				

(b) **Complete the sentences below.**

The original forecast trade receivables balance at the end of period 4 is £ [   ].

The revised forecast trade receivables balance at the end of period 4 is £ [   ].

A company is considering a marketing campaign to increase demand for its product. The marketing campaign will cost £2 million over a two month period. The sales are expected to increase by £300,000 per month from month 3 onwards. In anticipation of the demand increase the company will increase inventory levels in months 1-3 by £200,000 per month. Inventory will be paid for in the month following purchase, the marketing campaign will be paid for in month 2 and the sales are received in the month following sale.

(c) **Calculate the effect the above will have on the cash flow of the company in months 1 to 3.**

The cumulative cash flow for months 1-3 will [▼] by £ [   ] .

Drop-down list:

increase

reduce

Task 6 (12 marks)

The budgeted and actual cash flows for an organisation are summarised in the table below.

	Budgeted £	Actual £	Variance £	A/F
RECEIPTS				
Cash sales	25,000	75,300	50,300	F
Credit sales	275,000	175,470	99,530	A
Total receipts	300,000	250,770		
PAYMENTS				
Cash purchases	12,000	17,200	5,200	A
Credit purchases	125,000	135,000	10,000	A
Wages and salaries	42,700	42,700	0	0
Other expenses	3,500	7,500	4,000	A
Capital expenditure	50,000	0	50,000	F
Total payments	233,200	202,400		
Net cash flow	66,800	48,370		

The following information has been provided by a colleague.

- An existing customer who until recently had a good trading history appears to be suffering from cash flow problems. They were therefore required to pay cash for their purchases. The amount of cash purchases in the month from this customer was £45,000.

- The credit control manager was on sick leave during the month. She normally organises the credit control calls for her two assistants. In her absence her assistant produced an aged trade receivables analysis and used this to contact customers.

- The company has been increasing inventory levels over the past few months. The original budget expected inventory levels to remain constant.

- The company had planned to upgrade some plant and equipment during the period. However, the supplier had production problems and the delivery of the order has been delayed.

Identify FOUR significant variances for the period. Provide possible reasons why the variance might have occurred, suggest corrective actions where appropriate and identify implications for future budget setting.

Task 7 (12 marks)

(a) **Complete the following sentence.**

In times of recession banks often....

Increase the availability of loans and overdrafts.	☐
Convert overdrafts to loans to obtain a fixed charge.	☐
Convert loans to overdrafts to increase interest earned.	☐
Restrict the availability of loans and overdrafts.	☐

The following information has been gathered for the year ended 31 December 20X4.

	31 December 20X4
Gross profit	£647,875
Trade receivables	£450,000
Trade payables	£316,050
Trade receivables collection period in days	90
Inventory holding period in days	60

(b) **Complete the table below.**

	31 December 20X4
Sales revenue	
Cost of sales	
Inventories level in the statement of financial position	
Trade payables payment period in days	

(c) **Using your answers from part (b) calculate the cash operating cycle for the company.**

The cash operating cycle for the company is ☐ days.

Task 8 (12 marks)

(a) **Which of the following best describes a capped rate of interest?**

An interest rate that is guaranteed not to exceed a specified level. ☐

An interest rate that remains the same for the period of borrowing. ☐

An interest charge that is linked to capital interest rates. ☐

An interest rate that fluctuates in line with an agreed indicator. ☐

A company invests £120,000 in shares of a quoted company X. X has 35 million £1 shares in issue. The current market price of X's share is £3.84. The company's operating profit in 20X3 was £13.67 million. The dividend paid to shareholders was 25p per share.

(b) **Calculate the dividend yield for X.**

The dividend yield is [ ] %.

A company invests £120,000 in a fixed interest deposit account for three years. The rate of interest is 3%.

(c) **Calculate the balance in the account after three years if the interest is paid annually at the end of each year and the interest received remains in the account.**

The balance in the account at the end of three years is £ [ ].

A bank has offered to lend a company £135,000 at a flat rate of interest of 5.8% to be repaid over 36 months in equal instalments.

(d) **Calculate the monthly repayment of capital and interest.**

The monthly repayment of capital and interest is £ [ ].

An auction of 8% Treasury Stock 20X3 was undertaken by the UK DMO. The nominal (face value) of the Gilt is £100. A company purchased £200,000 nominal value at a price of £212,000.

(e) **Calculate how much interest the company will receive for each six month period and the interest yield (to two decimal places).**

The company will receive £ ⬚ interest every six months and the interest yield is ⬚ %.

Task 9 (16 marks)

The Finance Director has asked you to prepare some tutorial notes for use in training a junior colleague. The notes are to explain and illustrate how different types of leases can affect the company's statement of financial position, statement of profit or loss, gearing and credit rating.

Use the two types of leases below to prepare a tutorial note:

1. **Finance lease**
2 **Operating lease**

Tutorial notes

Task 10 (12 marks)

A company has £5,000,000 surplus cash which it is keen to invest for 5 years. The Finance Director has been tasked with preparing a Board Paper for discussion at the next Directing Board meeting. He has delegated this task to you, the Corporate Accountant.

Write a report to the Finance Director of the company which considers the risk, return and liquidity of each of the following investment options:

- **Land** which does not have planning permission, but on which the vendor has stated that planning consent is a certainty.

- **Long term fixed rate bond** with a leading UK bank, paying 3.5% interest per annum with early redemption penalties included in the conditions.

- **Investment in gold** in the form of purchasing Kruggerands or other readily tradeable gold coins.

Report to the Finance Director considering the risk, return and liquidity of investing in land, a long term fixed rate bond, and investing in gold coins.

AAT AQ2013 SAMPLE ASSESSMENT 2
CASH MANAGEMENT

ANSWERS

Cash Management (CSHM)

Task 1 (12 marks)

Use the table below to reconcile the opening cash position with the forecast closing cash position at 31 December 20X4. Use minus signs where appropriate.

	£
Operating profit	232,000
Change in inventories (W1)	−127,000
Change in trade receivables (W2)	−32,000
Change in trade payables (W3)	36,000
Adjustment for non-cash items (depreciation)	62,000
Purchase of non-current assets (W4)	−382,000
Tax paid (liability at end of 20X3 so paid in 20X4)	−55,000
Net change in cash position	−266,000
Forecast cash position 1 January 20X4 (taken from bal at 31 Dec 20X3)	212,000
Forecast cash position 31 December 20X4	−54,000

Workings

1. **Inventory**

   £357,000 − £230,000 = £127,000 (increase in inventory therefore deduct from operating profit)

2. **Receivables**

   £288,000 − £256,000 = £32,000 (increase in receivables therefore deduct from operating profit)

3. **Payables**

   £99,000 − £63,000 = £36,000 (increase in payables therefore add to operating profit)

4. **Non-current assets**

	£
Opening balance	480,000
Less depreciation	62,000
	418,000
Closing balance	800,000
Cash	382,000

Task 2 (14 marks)

(a) **Complete the table below, calculate the monthly sales volume trend and identify any monthly variations. Enter minus signs where appropriate, and round to the nearest whole number.**

Period	Sales volume (units)	Trend	Monthly variation (Volume less trend)
1	1,817		
2	1,650	1,705 (W1)	−55
3	1,648	1,806	−158
4	2,120	1,951	169
5	2,085	1,982	103
6	1,741	1,842	−101
7	1,700	1,885	−185
8	2,214		

(b) **Calculate the average monthly trend.** $\boxed{36}$ W2

Working

1. (1,817 + 1,650 + 1,648) / 3 = 1,705

2. (1,885 − 1,705) / 5 = 36

(c) **Assuming there is no monthly variation in months 15 and 16, calculate the forecast sales and complete the table below.**

Month 15 (units)	Month 16 (units)
2,135	2,170

Working

Month 15   2,065 + 35 + 35 = 2,135

Month 16   2,135 + 35 = 2,170

The selling price per unit is based on cost plus 40%.

The purchase price per unit in period 5 was £435 when the cost index was 145.

The cost index for period 16 is expected to be 180.

(d) **Calculate the selling price for period 16.**

£ 756

Working

$\dfrac{435}{145} \times 180 = 540$

$540 \times 1.4 = 756$

....

Task 3 (14 marks)

(a) **Complete the table below to identify the total sales receipts forecast for periods 5 and 6. Identify the forecast trade receivables balance at the end of period 3 and the irrecoverable debt provision for period 4.**

	Period 5 £	Period 6 £
Total sales receipts (W1)	138,480	141,780

The trade receivables balance at the end of period 3 is forecast to be:

£ 207,480 (W2)

The provision for irrecoverable debts for period 4 is forecast to be:

£ 7,080 (W3)

Workings

1. **Period 5 receipts**

Period 5 sales: 153,600 × 15%	=	23,040
Period 4 sales: 141,600 × 35%	=	49,560
Period 3 sales: 146,400 × 45%	=	65,880
Total	=	138,480

Period 6 receipts

Period 6 sales: 162,000 × 15%	=	24,300
Period 5 sales: 153,600 × 35%	=	53,760
Period 4 sales: 141,600 × 45%	=	63,720
Total	=	141,780

2. **Receivables (ie unpaid sales)**

Period 3 sales: 146,400 × (100% – 15%)	=	124,440
Period 2 sales: 151,200 × (100% – 15% – 35%)	=	75,600
Period 1 sales: 148,800 × (100% – 15% – 35% – 45%)	=	7,440 (irrecov debt)
Total	=	207,480

3.   141,600 × 5% = 7,080

Purchases

The company pays its suppliers on the basis of 45% one month after the date of purchase and 55% two months after the date of purchase.

(b) **At the end of period 3 the balance of trade payables is forecast to be:**

£ 128,017.50

Working

Period 2: 83,850 × 55%	=	46,117.50
Period 3:	=	81,900.00
	=	128,017.50

(c) **Complete the table below to identify the value of trade payables that will be paid in periods 4 and 5.**

	Period 4 £	Period 5 £
Settlement of trade payables	82,972.50	83,070

Workings

		Period 4 £	Period 5 £
Period 2	83,850 × 55%	46,117.50	
Period 3	81,900 × 45%	36,855.00	
	81,900 × 55%		45,045
Period 4	84,500 × 45%		38,025
		82,972.50	83,070

Task 4 (16 marks)

Using additional information above, complete the cash budget for the company for periods 6 and 7. Cash inflows should be entered as positive figures and cash outflows as negative figures (use brackets or minus signs). Round to the nearest whole £ throughout.

Cash Budget	Period 6 £	Period 7 £
RECEIPTS		
Sales receipts	2,403,332	2,198,462
Share issue (W1)	1,690,000	
Investment income (W2)		3,575
Rental income (W8)	1,400	1,400
Sale of non-current asset (W3)	13,170	
Total receipts	4,107,902	2,203,437
PAYMENTS		
Purchases	(1,432,096)	(950,132)
Wages and salaries	(526,636)	(492,713)
General expenses	(32,000)	(30,000)
Mortgage payment (W5)	−42,000	−42,000
VAT payment to HMRC (W7)	−144,000	0
Purchase of non-current assets (W4)	−46,400	−8,700
Dividend payment		−480,000
Overdraft interest (W9)	−8,400	
Total payments	−2,231,532	−2,003,545
Net cash flow	1,876,370	199,892
Opening bank balance	−840,000	1,036,370
Closing bank balance	1,036,370	1,236,262

Workings

1. 1.3m × £1.30 = £1,690,000

2. [£1.3m × (2.8% + 0.5%)] ÷ 12 = 3,575

3. NBV = cost – depreciation = £84,000 – (£84,000 × 75%) = £21,000

    Company made a loss of £7,830 ∴ cash received must have been £21,000 - £7,830 = £13,170

4. Purchase of asset: £116,000 × 40% = £46,400

    Instalments = (116,000 – 46,400) ÷ 8 = £8,700

5. Mortgage loan amount = £4,000,000 × 90% = £3,600,000

    Interest = £3,600,000 × (0.04 × 10 years) = £1,440,000

    Monthly payment = [(£3,600,000 + £1,440,000) ÷ 10 years] ÷ 12 months = £42,000

6. Dividend = 4,000,000 × £0.12 = £480,000

7. VAT = (£2,200,000 – £1,480,000) × 20% = £144,000

8. Rent = (£280,000 × 0.06) ÷ 12 = £1,400

9. Overdraft interest = £840,000 × (12%/12) = £8,400

Task 5 (16 marks)

(a) **Complete the table below to calculate the forecast sales receipts expected in periods 1 to 4 if the revised credit terms are offered.**

	Period 1 £	Period 2 £	Period 3 £	Period 4 £
Forecast sales receipts	0	0	1,650,000	2,882,000

Workings

£2,750,000 × 60% = £1,650,000

(£2,750,000 × 40%) + (£2,970,000 × 60%) = £2,882,000

(b) **Complete the sentences below.**

The original forecast trade receivables balance at the end of period 4 is £ ‹4,969,200›.

The revised forecast trade receivables balance at the end of period 4 is £ ‹7,326,000›.

Workings

£10,780,000 – £5,810,800 = £4,969,200

(£10,780,000 × 110%) – 2,882,000 – 1,650,000 = £7,326,000

(c) **Calculate the effect the above will have on the cash flow of the company in months 1 to 3.**

The cumulative cash flow for months 1 – 3 will [reduce ▼] by £ [2,400,000] .

Working

Marketing cost + 2 months inventory = £2,000,000 + £400,000 = £2,400,000

Task 6 (12 marks)

Identify FOUR significant variances for the period. Provide possible reasons why the variance might have occurred, suggest corrective actions where appropriate and identify implications for future budget setting.

<u>Cash sales</u>

- Main reason is that an existing customer had to pay on cash terms and £45,000 was received in the month.

- The remaining £5,300 could be for various reasons including:

  - New customers having to trade on cash terms.

  - There could have been an increase in sales volume or an increase in selling price.

  - Inaccurate forecasting.

Possible actions

- No action may be required if it is expected that the existing customer will revert to a credit customer in future periods. If not the budget figure may need to be revised for future periods.

<u>Credit sales</u>

Possible reasons

- Main reason is that an existing customer had to pay on cash terms so the credit sales would be lower and the cash received also lower.

- The credit control manager's absence may have resulted in inefficient chasing leading to lower collections.

Possible actions

- If sales volumes have not improved then it is possible that the favourable variance in this period will result in an adverse variance in subsequent periods and therefore future budgets should take this into consideration.

Credit purchases

Possible reason

- Main reason is that of increasing inventory levels which will increase purchases and hence increase payments.

Possible action

- The company could reduce inventory levels and therefore purchases and payments but if higher inventory levels are needed then the budget will need to be changed.

Capital expenditure

Possible reasons

- The only reason is that the delivery of the machine has been delayed due to the supplier's production problems.

Possible actions

- A new supplier could be sought if the current one cannot fulfil order.
- The future cape ex budgeted payments will need to be increased.

Task 7 (12 marks)

(a) **In times of recession banks often**

Increase the availability of loans and overdrafts.	☐
Convert overdrafts to loans to obtain a fixed charge.	☐
Convert loans to overdrafts to increase interest earned.	☐
Restrict the availability of loans and overdrafts.	☑

(b) **Complete the table below:**

	31 December 20X4
Sales revenue (W1)	1,825,000
Cost of sales (W2)	1,177,125
Inventories level in the statement of financial position (W3)	193,500
Trade payables payment period in days (W4)	98

Workings

1. Receivables collection period = (Trade receivables / credit sales) × 365

   ∴ 90 = (£450,000 / sales) × 365

   ∴ Sales = (£450,000 × 365) / 90 = £1,825,000

2. Sales – gross profit = cost of sales

   ∴ Cost of sales = £1,825,000 – £647,875 = £1,177,125

3. Inventory holding period = (Average inventory / cost of sales) × 365

   ∴ Average inventory = (60 × £1,177,125) / 365 = £193,500

4. Trade payables payment period = (Trade payables / credit purchases) × 365

   ∴ Trade payables payment period = (316,050 / 1,177,125) × 365 = 98 days

(c) **Using your answers from part (b) calculate the cash operating cycle for the company.**

The cash operating cycle for the company is ⌈ 52 ⌉ days.

Working

90 + 60 – 98 = 52

....

Task 8 (12 marks)

(a) **Which of the following best describes a capped rate of interest?**

An interest rate that is guaranteed not to exceed a specified level.	✓
An interest rate that remains the same for the period of borrowing.	☐
An interest charge that is linked to capital interest rates.	☐
An interest rate that fluctuates in line with an agreed indicator.	☐

A company invests £120,000 in shares of a quoted company X. X has 35 million £1 shares in issue. The current market price of X's share is £3.84. The company's operating profit in 20X3 was £13.67 million. The dividend paid to shareholders was 25p per share.

(b) **Calculate the dividend yield for X.**

The dividend yield is ⌈ 6.51 ⌉ %.

Working

Dividend yield = (Dividend per share / Market price per share) × 100%

∴ Dividend yield = (0.25 / £3.84) × 100% = 6.51%

A company invests £120,000 in a fixed interest deposit account for three years. The rate of interest is 3%.

(c) **Calculate the balance in the account after three years if the interest is paid annually at the end of each year and the interest received remains in the account.**

The balance in the account at the end of three years is £ 131,127.24 .

Working

£120,000 × 1.03³ = £131,127.24

A bank has offered to lend a company £135,000 at a flat rate of interest of 5.8% to be repaid over 36 months in equal instalments.

(d) **Calculate the monthly repayment of capital and interest.**

The monthly repayment of capital and interest is £ 4,402.50 .

Working

Interest = £135,000 × 0.058 × 3 years = £23,490

Monthly repayment = (£135,000 + £23,490) / 36 = £4,402.50

An auction of 8% Treasury Stock 20X3 was undertaken by the UK DMO. The nominal (face value) of the Gilt is £100. A company purchased £200,000 nominal value at a price of £212,000.

(e) **Calculate how much interest the company will receive for each six month period and the interest yield (to two decimal places).**

The company will receive £ 8,000 interest every six months and the interest yield is 7.55 %.

Working

(£200,000 × 8%) / 2 = £8,000

Yield = (£16,000 / £212,000) × 100% = 7.55%

Task 9 (16 marks)

Use the two types of leases below to prepare a tutorial note:

1. Finance lease
2. Operating lease

Tutorial notes

Leases

- There are two main types of leases; a finance lease and an operating lease.
- The key difference is who has access to the "RISK AND REWARD" of the asset.

- An operating lease is where the risk and reward is substantially retained by the lessor and the lessee is effectively renting the asset.

- An operating lease is not recognised on the statement of financial position, but has to be shown in a note detailing the annual commitments which cannot be cancelled.

- An operating lease is 'off balance sheet'.

- The statement of profit or loss will include the "rental" payments as an expense.

- The payments will be spread over the term of the lease so cash outflows will be spread over (say) 5 years for a 5 year lease.

- The gearing of the company will be unaffected as the lease is "off balance sheet".

- Therefore the total debt on the balance sheet will be unaffected by the lease and the asset value is also unaffected, but a competent credit risk analyst will consider the size of the lease commitment and estimate a revised gearing position based upon including the operating lease as finance.

- A finance lease is where the risk and reward is substantially transferred to the lessee as if the lessee has purchased the asset with a loan.

- A finance lease has to be shown on the statement of financial position by capitalising the asset and including the loan element of the lease as borrowing.

- The finance lease includes implicit interest charges which will be charged as an expense in the statement of profit or loss.

- The cash balance will not be affected by the acquisition but will be reduced by the lease payments.

- The payments will be spread over the term of the lease (which could be 5 years), aiding short term cash flow.

- The gearing of the company will increase because the asset base increases but so does the total debt.

- The increase in gearing could affect the company's ability to raise additional finance.

- The net assets will be unchanged at acquisition but the debt will increase.

- The statement of profit or loss will recognise the interest element of the finance lease payments but not the capital repayment element.

- However, the asset will be depreciated over the lease term, or perhaps longer if the UEL is greater. Therefore a depreciation charge will go to P&L.

Task 10 (12 marks)

Report to the Finance Director considering the risk, return and liquidity of investing in land, a long term fixed rate bond, and investing in gold coins.

<u>Land</u>

Risk

- This is high risk as the return is unknown and uncertain.

- Historically land is deemed to be a fairly safe investment as there is a finite supply, however, there is uncertainty surrounding the value to a developer.

- Therefore there is a risk to the return and also to the initial investment.

Return

- If the planning permission is granted the value of the land could increase considerably.

- On the other hand if planning permission is refused then the value of the land could reduce considerably.

- In the last decade land values have been volatile sometimes resulting in a substantial capital loss for investors.

- However, with planning permission the land will have a value and it is likely that a gain will be made.

- There will be additional costs (eg legal, planning fees, advertising etc) in both the acquisition and disposal.

- But there is always a chance that the sales value will be less than the purchases cost.

Liquidity

- Land is one of the least liquid assets due to the time it can take to sell and complete the transaction, which can take months.

- In the case where cash is needed quickly the price may have to be significantly reduced to secure a sale.

<u>Long term bank deposit</u>

Risk

- It is difficult to identify the risk on this investment as the interest rate is fixed and the return is guaranteed.

- Historically banks were seen as safe investments.

- However, that has changed and although governments have bailed out banks some may still fail.

- Traditionally fixed rate accounts were seen as risk free from the perspective of the loss of capital value. However in light of the global financial crisis there is a risk of loss of capital value if the deposit is not covered by a government backed guarantee scheme.

- There is a risk that early redemption penalties may be imposed but this is usually a couple of month's interest and there is no risk to the capital.

Return

- The return is 3.5% per annum which is lower than the expected return on the land. This return should be guaranteed assuming it is a large UK bank which will be supported by the UK government.

- The initial investment of £500,000 is also guaranteed.

Liquidity

- The liquidity will be dependent on the terms of the investment. The investment is for a fixed period, however it may be possible to redeem the investment early with a small interest penalty.

- Therefore the investment is readily available.

<u>Gold Coins</u>

Risk

- Investment in gold coins may be considered high risk as the price of gold can fluctuate.

- Historically gold prices have increased but recently the price of gold has dropped substantially (by 25%).

- As there is a finite supply of gold, and the commodity is becoming scarcer and more expensive to extract, the possibility is that gold prices may increase.

- However, there has been a substantial increase in gold prices since the 2008 global financial crisis with many investors seeking a commodity not associated with a single economy.

- Some experts believe that long term gold prices will hit £2,000 an ounce yet equally as many believe long term gold prices will fall.

Return

- The return achievable cannot be identified with any certainty at the time of investment because the gold market fluctuates daily.

- There may be additional storage costs.

- There may be increased insurance premiums if the gold is kept on the company premises.

- There may be broker charges for acquisition and sale.

Liquidity

- Gold coins are tradable so liquidity is high. It would take only a few days for the company to realise its cash as long as it is prepared to take the price offered at that point in time.

- The company could also realise its cash piecemeal as and when required by selling any number of gold coins it holds.

- Therefore liquidity is good but return may be uncertain due to the volatility of the gold market.

BPP PRACTICE ASSESSMENT 1
CASH MANAGEMENT

Time allowed: 2.5 hours

Task 1

(a) **Complete the table by ticking the correct boxes to show whether an item affects cash or profit.**

	Cash	Profit
Purchases on credit		
Purchase of non-current asset		
Prepayment of expenses		
Depreciation		
Payments to credit suppliers		
Payment into a business by its owner		

(b) There are many different types of cash flows.

Complete the table below by dragging and dropping the correct description to match the type of cash receipt or cash payment.

Transaction	Type of receipt or payment
Payments to suppliers	
Dividend	
Sale of non-current assets	
Receipts from cash customers	
Payment of wages	
Payment of insurance claim for damage caused by goods sold	

Regular
Irregular
Capital
Exceptional

(c) Extracts from a company's statement of profit or loss and statement of financial position are given below. These are prepared on an accruals basis and the business holds minimal inventory.

Summarised statement of profit or loss for three months to 31 March

	£	£
Sales revenue		200,340
Less purchases		(119,500)
Gross profit		80,840
Less expenses		
Wages	22,500	
Rent of office	18,000	
Office expenses	7,400	
Van expenses	6,800	
Van depreciation	3,200	
		(57,900)
		22,940

Extracts from the statements of financial position at 1 January and 31 March show the following:

Statement of Financial Position at	31 March	1 January
	£	£
Trade receivables	20,100	25,600
Trade payables	4,800	2,100
Accruals – office expenses	500	350
Prepayments – van expenses	700	200
Prepayments – rent of office	3,000	2,000

Calculate the actual business cash receipts and cash payments for the quarter to 31 March.

	£
Sales receipts	
Purchases payments	
Wages paid	
Rent paid	
Office expenses	
Van expenses	
Van depreciation	

Task 2

(a) A company uses an industry wage rate index to forecast future monthly wage costs. The current monthly wage cost of £10,660 was calculated when the wage index was 110. The forecast wage index for June is 144.

If the company uses the forecast wage rate index, what will the wage cost for June be to the nearest £?

£15,350 ☐

£8,143 ☐

£13,955 ☐

£11,726 ☐

(b) A business has access to the following sources of information:

(i)   Market data on average wage rises and inflation rates
(ii)   Industry information on competitors' labour costs
(iii)   Data on the labour costs of key suppliers
(iv)   Production department's labour usage budget
(v)   Current payroll information from HR department

Which are likely to be the most useful in forecasting the total cost of labour for the business?

(i), (iii) and (v) ☐

(i), (iv) and (v) ☐

(ii), (iv) and (v) ☐

All of the above ☐

(c) **Complete the sentences below using the picklists.**

Time series analysis is used in budgeting to estimate future figures based upon a past trend. A (1) [▾] can be used to determine the trend in a time series. The trend is the general (2) [▾] movement of the time series. In the additive model future figures can be budgeted by adjusting the trend for any (3) [▾]. The process of using historical information to estimate future figures is known as (4) [▾] This assumes that the trend and any seasonal variations (5) [▾] in the future.

Picklist:

Cyclical average/moving average/multiplicative average

Short-term/long-term

Seasonal variation/random variation

Extrapolation/interpolation

Will apply/won't apply

. . . .

Task 3

PL Ltd is a company which manufactures fence panels. Production is budgeted to be 7,100 units in July, 7,300 units in August and 7,600 units in September.

You are given the following information regarding the purchases for the company:

(1) The cost of a strip of wood is expected to remain at £0.20 per strip for the next six months.

(2) Each fence panel requires 25 strips of wood.

(3) Wood inventory at 30 June 20X6 are 160,000 strips valued at £32,000.

(4) The plan is to reduce inventory of wood to 150,000 strips at the end of August and 120,000 strips at the end of September.

(a) **Complete the table below to calculate the purchases budget in units and in £ for the three-month period ending in September.**

	Workings	July	August	September
		Strips of wood	Strips of wood	Strips of wood
Production requirements				
Opening inventory				
Closing inventory				
Purchases in units				
		£	£	£
Purchases in £				

All purchases of wood will continue to be paid for one month in arrears as at present. The payables amount at 30 June 20X6 for purchases of wood made during June was £33,500.

(b) **Complete the table below to calculate the payments made to suppliers in each of the three months ending in September.**

	Workings	July £	August £	September £

Each panel takes 20 minutes of labour time to manufacture and the production staff are currently paid £7.50 per hour. It is expected that this will increase to £7.80 per hour from 1 September 20X6.

(c) **Complete the table below to calculate the wages cost for each of the three months ending in September.**

	Workings	July £	August £	September £

Task 4

The cash budget for GI Ltd for the three months ended September has been partially completed. The following information is to be incorporated and the cash budget completed.

Additional information

- Fixed production overheads are expected to remain at £14,000 for July 20X6 which includes £4,000 of depreciation. The overheads other than depreciation are expected to increase by 5% from 1 August 20X6.

- Repairs and maintenance costs should be budgeted at an average of £2,500 per month.

- Sales department costs are expected to be £4,000 per month including depreciation of £800 per month.

- Capital expenditure of £20,000 should be budgeted for in August 20X6.

- The cash balance at 30 June 20X6 was £23,900.

Using the additional information above, complete the cash budget for GI Ltd for the three months ending in September. Cash inflows should be entered as positive figures and cash outflows as negative figures. Zeroes must be entered where appropriate to achieve full marks.

Cash budget for three months ending 30 September 20X6

	July £	August £	September £
Receipts:			
Receipts from customers	**104,697**	**106,284**	**109,296**
Payments:			
Payments to suppliers	−50,200	−52,600	−51,400
Wages	−21,300	−21,900	−23,700
Production overheads			
Selling overheads			
Repairs and maintenance			
Capital expenditure			
Total payments:			
Net cash flow			
Opening cash balance			
Closing cash balance			

Task 5

A cash budget has been prepared for KL Ltd for the next five periods.

The budget was prepared based on the following sales volumes and a selling price of £10 per item.

	Period 1	Period 2	Period 3	Period 4	Period 5
Sales volume (items)	1,400	1,500	1,450	1,390	1,300

The pattern of cash receipts used in the budget assumed 60% of sales were paid for by customers in the month following the sale and the remaining 40% of customers paid two months after the sale.

The company is considering introducing a settlement discount of 2% for payments made in the month of the sale. This policy is expected to result in 50% of customers paying in the month of the sale, 10% paying in the month following the sale and the remaining 40% paying two months following the sale.

(a) **Complete the table below to calculate the forecast receipts from customers for each of periods 3, 4 and 5 under the current payment system from customers.**

	Workings	Period 3 £	Period 4 £	Period 5 £
Total receipts from customers				

(b) **Complete the table below to calculate the forecast receipts from customers for each of periods 3, 4 and 5 if the system of settlement discounts is introduced.**

	Workings	Period 3 £	Period 4 £	Period 5 £
Total receipts from customers				

(c) **Complete the table below to show the effects of introducing the discount system.**

	Period 3 £	Period 4 £	Period 5 £
Original receipts from customers			
Revised receipts from customers			
Increase/(decrease) in sales receipts			

Task 6

(a) Given below is the cash budget for the three months ended 30 June 20X6 for an organisation. You are also given the actual cash flows for the three-month period.

Cash budget for the three months ended 30 June 20X6

	April £	May £	June £
Receipts from customers	91,500	96,700	92,400
Payments to suppliers	−31,400	−28,800	−30,100
Wages	−16,250	−16,500	−16,750
Production overheads	−10,000	−10,000	−10,000
Selling overheads	−3,300	−3,000	−3,000
Repairs and maintenance	−1,100	−1,500	−1,100
Capital expenditure	0	0	0
Dividend	−	−	−30,000
Cash flow for the month	29,450	36,900	1,450
Opening cash balance	41,100	70,550	107,450
Closing cash balance	70,550	107,450	108,900

Actual cash flows

The actual cash flows for each of the three months ended 30 June 20X6 were as follows:

	April £	May £	June £
Receipts from customers	86,500	91,200	84,400
Payments to suppliers	−33,200	−33,200	−32,700
Wages	−16,250	−16,500	−16,750
Production overheads	−10,000	−10,000	−10,000
Selling overheads	−3,100	−3,400	−3,500
Repairs and maintenance	−4,100	−3,900	−2,700
Capital expenditure		−50,000	
Dividend	−	−	−30,000
Cash flow for the month	19,850	−25,800	11,250
Opening cash balance	41,100	60,950	35,150
Closing cash balance	60,950	35,150	23,900

Prepare a reconciliation of the budgeted cash balance with the actual cash balance at 30 June 20X6. Select the appropriate description for each entry by highlighting it. Clearly indicate whether figures are to be added or deducted in the reconciliation by entering minus signs where appropriate.

	£
Budgeted closing cash balance	
Surplus/shortfall in receipts from customers	
Increase/decrease in payments to suppliers	
Increase/decrease in selling overheads	
Increase/decrease in repairs and maintenance	
Increase/decrease in capital expenditure	
Actual closing cash balance	

(b) **For each of the following significant deviations from a cash budget suggest one possible course of action that could have been taken to avoid the variance.**

> Deviation in receipts from customers

> Deviation in payments to suppliers

> Change in repairs and maintenance payments

> Change in capital expenditure

Task 7

(a) XYZ Ltd currently has a cash operating cycle of 35 days. It plans to introduce a new product range which will increase the inventory holding period by 5 days and increase the time taken to collect cash from customers by 14 days.

What is the new cash operating cycle? [ ] days.

(b) **The cash operating cycle is the period of time that a business takes to pay its suppliers.**

True [ ]

False [ ]

(c) **Complete the sentences below using the picklists.**

A business that is overcapitalised has (1) [▼] working capital for the scale of its operations. It is likely to have an (2) [▼] in current assets and make (3) [▼] use of credit from suppliers.

Picklist:

Too much/too little
Over-investment/under-investment
Sufficient/insufficient

Task 8

A firm is planning to expand its production facilities. The expansion plans will require the purchase of new machinery at a cost of £50,000 and additional working capital of £20,000.

The following finance options are available:

Option 1

A bank loan of £50,000 secured on the new machinery, with a flat rate of interest of 7% p.a. The loan principal plus the total interest on the loan is to be repaid in four equal annual instalments.

The bank is also offering an overdraft facility of £20,000 which attracts an annual interest rate of 10%. The firm believe that they will require an overdraft for the first two years only, with an average balance of £10,000 in year 1 and £8,000 in year 2. Annual overdraft interest will be charged on the last day of the year.

Option 2

A bank loan of £75,000 secured with a floating charge on the firm's assets.

There is a capital repayment holiday for the first year and then capital is to be repaid in three equal instalments at the end of the second, third and fourth years.

An arrangement fee of £1,000 will be charged and is payable at the end of the first year.

The interest rate is fixed at 7.5% per annum. Interest is charged on the last day of the year, on the capital amount outstanding at the start of the year.

Under this option there will be no requirement for a bank overdraft facility.

Complete the tables below to compare the total finance cost of the two options and the timing of the payments.

	Loan interest £	Overdraft interest £	Arrangement fee £	Total cost £
Option 1				
Option 2				

	Year 1	Year 2	Year 3	Year 4
Option 1 Finance costs				
Option 1 Capital repayments				
Total Option 1				

	Year 1	Year 2	Year 3	Year 4
Option 2 Finance costs				
Option 2 Capital repayments				
Total Option 2				

Task 9

The following financial information relates to ABC Co:

	20X7 £'000	20X6 £'000
Statement of Profit or Loss		
Sales (all on credit)	37,400	26,720
Cost of sales	34,408	23,781
Operating profit	2,992	2,939
Finance costs (interest payments)	355	274
Profit before taxation	2,637	2,665
Statement of Financial Position		
Non-current assets	13,632	12,750
Current assets		
Inventory	4,600	2,400
Trade receivables	4,600	2,200
	9,200	4,600
Total assets	22,832	17,350
Capital and reserves		
Share capital	6,000	6,000
Reserves	6,432	5,325
	12,432	11,325
Current liabilities		
Trade payables	4,750	2,000
Overdraft	3,225	1,600
	7,975	3,600
Non-current liabilities		
8% Bonds	2,425	2,425
Total equity and liabilities	22,832	17,350

The average variable overdraft interest rate in each year was 5%. A factor has offered to take over the administration of trade receivables on a non-recourse basis for an annual fee of 3% of credit sales. The factor will maintain a trade receivables collection period of 30 days and ABC Co will save £100,000 per year in administration costs and £350,000 per year in irrecoverable debts. A condition of the factoring agreement is that the factor would advance 80% of the face value of receivables at an annual interest rate of 7%.

Prepare notes for a report, using the above financial information to discuss, with supporting calculations,

(i)   **Whether or not ABC Co is overtrading.**

(ii) **Whether the proposal to factor trade receivables is financially acceptable. Assume an average cost of short-term finance of 5%.**

Task 10

A company has a cash surplus of £75,000 available to invest for eighteen months before the capital will be required to construct a new production line.

The cash is currently held in a bank deposit account.

The company has decided to consider the following two options for its investment:

Option 1:

Invest in a mixed portfolio of shares and treasury stock. The minimum period of investment is 6 months; interest rate is 6% p.a.

Option 2:

Invest in a deposit account with an interest rate is 5% p.a.. There is a penalty of 1% of capital invested for withdrawal before 12 months and a bonus of 2% of capital invested if the deposit is held for more than twelve months. At the end of the first year the bonus will be added to the capital amount and interest will be payable on the increased amount.

Prepare an email to the finance director of the company comparing the risk and return of the two options and recommending a course of action for the company.

BPP PRACTICE ASSESSMENT 1
CASH MANAGEMENT

ANSWERS

Task 1

(a)

	Cash	Profit
Purchases on credit		✓
Purchase of non-current asset	✓	
Prepayment of expenses		✓
Depreciation		✓
Payments to credit suppliers	✓	
Payment into a business by its owner	✓	

(b)

Transaction	Type of receipt or payment
Payments to suppliers	Regular
Dividend	Capital
Sale of non-current assets	Capital
Receipts from cash customers	Regular
Payment of wages	Regular
Payment of insurance claim for damage caused by goods sold	Exceptional

(c)

	£
Sales receipts	205,840
Purchases payments	116,800
Wages paid	22,500
Rent paid	19,000
Office expenses	7,250
Van expenses	7,300
Van depreciation	0

Workings

Sales receipts	= 200,340 + 25,600 – 20,100	= 205,840
Purchases payments	= 119,500 + 2,100 – 4,800	= 116,800
Rent paid	= 18,000 – 2,000 + 3,000	= 19,000
Office expenses	= 7,400 + 350 – 500	= 7,250
Van expenses	= 6,800 – 200 + 700	= 7,300
Van depreciation	= 0 (this is not a cash expense)	

Task 2

(a) The correct answer is £13,955

£10,660 × 144/110 = £13,955

(b) The correct answer is (i), (iv) and (v)

(c) Time series analysis is used in budgeting to estimate future figures based upon a past trend. A (1) | moving average | can be used to determine the trend in a time series. The trend is the general (2) | long-term | movement of the time series. In the additive model future figures can be budgeted by adjusting the trend for any (3) | seasonal variation |. The process of using historical information to estimate future figures is known as (4) | extrapolation |. This assumes that the trend and any seasonal variations (5) | will apply | in the future.

Task 3

(a) Purchases budget

	Workings	July	August	September
		Strips of wood	Strips of wood	Strips of wood
Production requirements	7,100 × 25	177,500		
	7,300 × 25		182,500	
	7,600 × 25			190,000
Opening inventory		−160,000	−160,000	−150,000
Closing inventory		160,000	150,000	120,000
Purchases in units		**177,500**	**172,500**	**160,000**
		£	£	£
Purchases in £ (units × £0.20)		**35,500**	**34,500**	**32,000**

(b) Payments to suppliers

	Workings	July £	August £	September £
Opening payable		33,500		
July purchases			35,500	
August purchases				34,500

(c) Wages payments

	Workings	July £	August £	September £
July	7,100/3 × £7.50	17,750		
August	7,300/3 × £7.50		18,250	
September	7,600/3 × £7.80			19,760

Task 4

Cash budget for three months ending 30 September 20X6

	July £	August £	September £
Receipts:			
Receipts from customers	**104,697**	**106,284**	**109,296**
Payments:			
Payments to suppliers	−50,200	−52,600	−51,400
Wages	−21,300	−21,900	−23,700
Production overheads	−10,000	−10,500	−10,500
Selling overheads	−3,200	−3,200	−3,200
Repairs and maintenance	−2,500	−2,500	−2,500
Capital expenditure	0	−20,000	0
Total payments:	**−87,200**	**−110,700**	**−91,300**
Net cash flow	17,497	−4,416	17,996
Opening cash balance	23,900	41,397	36,981
Closing cash balance	41,397	36,981	54,977

Task 5

(a)

	Period 3 £	Period 4 £	Period 5 £
Period 1 sales 1,400 × £10 × 40%	5,600		
Period 2 sales 1,500 × £10 × 60%	9,000		
Period 2 sales 1,500 × £10 × 40%		6,000	
Period 3 sales 1,450 × £10 × 60%		8,700	
Period 3 sales 1,450 × £10 × 40%			5,800
Period 4 sales 1,390 × £10 × 60%			8,340
Total receipts from customers	**14,600**	**14,700**	**14,140**

(b)

	Period 3 £	Period 4 £	Period 5 £
Period 1 sales 1,400 × £10 × 40%	5,600		
Period 2 sales 1,500 × £10 × 10%	1,500		
Period 3 sales 1,450 × £10 × 50% × 98%	7,105		
Period 2 sales 1,500 × £10 × 40%		6,000	
Period 3 sales 1,450 × £10 × 10%		1,450	
Period 4 sales 1,390 × £10 × 50% × 98%		6,811	
Period 3 sales 1,450 × £10 × 40%			5,800
Period 4 sales 1,390 × £10 × 10%			1,390
Period 5 sales 1,300 × £10 × 50% × 98%			6,370
Total receipts from customers	**14,205**	**14,261**	**13,560**

(c)

	Period 3 £	Period 4 £	Period 5 £
Original receipts from customers	14,600	14,700	14,140
Revised receipts from customers	14,205	14,261	13,560
Increase/(decrease) in sales receipts	−395	−439	−580

Task 6

(a)

	£
Budgeted closing cash balance	108,900
Shortfall in receipts from customers	−18,500
Increase in payments to suppliers	−8,800
Increase in selling overheads	−700
Increase in repairs and maintenance	−7,000
Increase in capital expenditure	−50,000
Actual closing cash balance	23,900

(b)

Deviation in receipts from customers	Improve credit control procedures
Deviation in payments to suppliers	Negotiate better price or credit terms for payment
Change in repairs and maintenance payments	Arrange a fixed price maintenance contract
Change in capital expenditure	Delay expenditure or find an alternative method of (such as leasing)

Task 7

(a) 54 days

   (35 + 5 + 14 = 54)

(b) False

   The cash operating cycle is the period of time between cash being paid for raw materials and cash being received from customers for goods sold.

(c) A business that is overcapitalised has (1) [Too much] working capital for the scale of its operations. It is likely to have an (2) [Over-investment] in current assets and make (3) [insufficient] use of credit from suppliers.

Task 8

	Loan interest £	Overdraft interest £	Arrangement fee £	Total cost £
Option 1	14,000	1,800	0	15,800
Option 2	16,875	0	1,000	17,875

	Year 1	Year 2	Year 3	Year 4
Option 1 Finance costs	4,500	4,300	3,500	3,500
Option 1 Capital repayments	12,500	12,500	12,500	12,500
Total Option 1	17,000	16,800	16,000	16,000

	Year 1	Year 2	Year 3	Year 4
Option 2 Finance costs	6,625	5,625	3,750	1,875
Option 2 Capital repayments	0	25,000	25,000	25,000
Total Option 2	6,625	30,625	28,750	26,875

Task 9

(i) Overtrading

Overtrading happens when a business tries to do too much too quickly with too little long-term capital, so that it is trying to support too large a volume of trade with the capital resources at its disposal. Even if an overtrading business operates at a profit, it could easily run into serious trouble because it is short of money. Such liquidity troubles stem from the fact that it does not have enough capital to provide the cash to pay its debts as they fall due.

Symptoms of overtrading are as follows.

A rapid increase in turnover

ABC Co has experienced a 40% increase in turnover from 20X6 to 20X7 and net working capital has not increased in line. The sales/net working capital ratio has increased from 26.72 times to 30.53 times.

A rapid increase in the volume of current assets

Inventories have increased by 92% and receivables by 109%. Inventory turnover has slowed down, with 12 more days of inventory held and the accounts receivable collection period has increased by 15 days. So the rate of increase in inventories and accounts receivable has been even greater than the rate of increase in sales. Inventory may have been stockpiled in anticipation of a further increase in turnover. The increase in sales could have partly arisen due to a relaxation of credit terms for receivables.

Most of the increase in assets is financed by credit

The payment period for accounts payable has lengthened from 31 days to 50 and there has been an overall increase of 138% in payables. The bank overdraft has also increased by 102%.

Falling liquidity ratios

Both the current ratio and the quick ratio have deteriorated.

Conclusion

There is clear evidence that ABC Co is overtrading. It would be helpful to have benchmark information such as key ratios from similar companies and more information from prior years to see if there is definitely a trend.

(ii) Benefits

Current receivables	= £4,600,000	
Receivables under factor	= £37,400,000 × 30/365	= £3,073,973
Reduction in receivables	= £4,600,000 – £3,073,973	= £1,526,027
Reduction in finance cost	= 1,526,027 × 5% due to improved speed of collection	= £76,301 per year
Administration cost savings		= £100,000 per year
Bad debt savings		= £350,000 per year
Total savings		= £526,301 per year

Costs

Factor's annual fee = £37,400,000 × 3% = £1,122,000 per year

Extra interest cost on advance = £3,073,973 × 80% × (7% – 5%) = £49,184 per year

Total additional costs = £1,171,184 per year

The proposal to factor trade receivables is **not financially acceptable** as there is a net cost of £644,883 per year.

Calculations:

	20X7	20X6
Inventory days 4,600/34,408 × 365	= 49 days	2,400/23,781 × 365 = 37 days
Receivables days 4,600/37,400 × 365	= 45 days	2,200/26,720 × 365 = 30 days
Payables days 4,750/34,408 × 365	= 50 days	2,000/23,781 × 365 = 31 days
Current ratio 9,200/7,975	= 1.15 times	4,600/3,600 = 1.28 times
Quick ratio 4,600/7,975	= 0.58 times	2,200/3,600 = 0.61 times
Sales/net working capital	= 30.53 times	26,720/(4,600 – 3,600) =26.72 times

37,400/(9,200 – 7,975)

Increase in sales (37,400 – 26,720)/ 26,720 × 100% = 40%
Increase in non-current assets (13,632 – 12,750)/12,750 × 100% = 7%
Increase in net working capital (1,225 – 1,000)/1,000 = 22.5%
Increase in inventory (4,600 – 2,400)/2,400 × 100% = 92%
Increase in receivables (4,600 – 2,200)/2,200 × 100% = 109%
Increase in payables (4,750 – 2,000)/2,000 × 100% = 138%
Increase in overdraft (3,225 – 1,600)/1,600 × 100% = 102%

Task 10

Email		
To: fd@company.co.uk	**Date**:	Today
From: aatstudent@company.co.uk	**Subject**:	Investment options

The company has £75,000 to invest for a period of eighteen months. As the investment is required for the construction of the new production line, it is important that we do not expose the company to too much risk.

If the company selects Option 1, the total return on the investment will be **£6,750**.

If the company selects Option 2, the total return on the investment will be **£7,162.50**.

The risk is higher with Option 1 and the return is lower.

I recommend that **Option 2** be selected as this will have the **highest return** for the company and the **lowest risk**. The return on investment for the eighteen month period will be **9.55%** (as opposed to 9% with Option 1).

Workings:

Option 1: £75,000 × 6% × 18/12 = £6,750

Option 2:

Interest year 1 = £75,000 × 5% = £3,750

Bonus = 2% × £75,000 = £1,500

Interest year 2 = 5% × £76,500 × 6/12 = £1,912.50

Total Option 2 = £3,750 + £1,500 + £1,912.50 = £7,162.50

Increase return of £7,162.50/£75,000 = 9.55%

BPP PRACTICE ASSESSMENT 2
CASH MANAGEMENT

Time allowed: 2.5 hours

PRACTICE ASSESSMENT 2

Task 1

The accountant of a company has prepared a budgeted statement of profit or loss for the month of April 20X6 and a statement of financial position as at 30 April 20X6.

Extracts from the statement of profit or loss are as follows:

	£
Sales revenue	170,000
Purchases	72,000
Factory rent	31,000
Administrative expenses	14,000
Delivery lorry expenses	16,000
Delivery lorry depreciation	3,000

Extracts from the statement of financial position at 1 April and 30 April are as follows:

	30 April		1 April	
Receivables	39,000		32,000	
Payables	15,000		17,000	
Prepaid factory rent	7,000		6,000	
Accrued administrative expenses	2,000		1,000	
Accrued delivery lorry expenses	4,000		2,000	

Calculate the actual cash receipts and payments for the month of April.

	£
Receipts for sales	
Payments for purchases	
Factory rent paid	
Administrative expenses paid	
Delivery lorry expenses paid	
Depreciation	

Task 2

A company is trying to estimate its production volumes for one of its products for the first three months of 20X6. This to be done by calculating a trend using the actual monthly production volumes for 20X5 and a 3-point moving average.

(a) **Complete the table below to calculate the monthly production volume trend and identify any monthly variations.**

	Production volume Units	Trend Units	Monthly variation (volume less trend) Units
January	90,000		
February	98,000		
March	112,000		
April	96,000		
May	104,000		
June	118,000		
July	102,000		
August	110,000		
September	124,000		
October	108,000		
November	116,000		
December	130,000		

The monthly sales volume trend is [   ] units.

(b) **Using the trend and the monthly variations identified in part (a) complete the table below for forecast sales volume for January, February and March of the next financial year.**

	Forecast trend Units	Variation Units	Forecast sales volume Units
January			
February			
March			

Task 3

Happy Chefs Ltd, a catering company providing catering and meals for corporate and private clients, is preparing its cash budget for the first three months of 20X6.

January credit sales will be £104,000, February should be £140,000 and March £155,000. Cash inflows from sales invoices will be as follows:

- 40% in the month the invoice is issued
- 50% in the month after the invoice is issued
- 10% two months after the invoice is issued

Receivables at 31 December 20X5 were £160,000 and of these it is anticipated that £125,000 will be received in January and the remainder in February.

From 1 February the company is opening a factory sales outlet for sales to the public of pre-packaged foods. In the early months sales for cash are expected to total £800 a month.

Complete the table below to calculate the receipts from sales for the three months ending in March.

	Workings	January £	February £	March £
Cash sales				
Opening receivables				
January sales				
February sales				
March sales				
Total receipts from sales				

Task 4

Happy Chefs Ltd needs to complete a budget for cash payments for the first three months of 20X6. It estimates that on average it earns a gross margin of 40% on the sale of meals and catering. The total cost of each meal is made up of 30% ingredients and 70% labour and overheads. The suppliers of ingredients are always paid one month after the month of purchase. Because ingredients are perishable, inventory is kept to a minimum.

Labour and overheads are paid in the month incurred.

Trade payables at 1 January 20X6 are £17,600.

(a) **Complete the table below to calculate cost of sales for the three months from January to March:**

	Workings	January £	February £	March £
Total sales		104,000	140,800	155,800
Cost of sales				
Split:				
Ingredients				
Labour and overheads				

(b) **Complete the table below to calculate the cash payments made in each of the three months:**

	January £	February £	March £	Trade payables at 31 March £
Payment to suppliers				
Payment for labour and overheads				
Total cash payments				

Task 5

A company is preparing its cash budget for the first three months of 20X6. The following information is known regarding forecast cash payments. The receipts have already been calculated and are given in the cash budget below.

- Purchases were £70,000 in December and are expected to be £41,600 in January, £56,000 in February and £62,000 in March. These purchases are paid for in the month after purchase.

- Salaries are currently £43,000 but are due to rise by 5% from 1 March.

- Administration costs will be £27,000 in January but due to a rent increase will go up by £3,000 from 1 February onwards.

- The company is investing in new equipment and there is to be a down payment of £20,000 on 1 February and a monthly payment thereafter of £6,000.

- The cash balance at 31 December 20X5 was an overdraft of £39,400 (ignore any interest on the overdraft.)

Prepare a monthly cash budget for the company for the three months to March.

	January £	February £	March £
Cash receipts			
Receipts from sales	153,400	148,800	145,600
Deposit account interest	100	100	100
Total cash receipts	**153,500**	**148,900**	**145,700**
Cash payments			
Payments to suppliers			
Salaries			
Administration overheads			
Capital expenditure			
Total payments			
Net cash flow			
Opening cash balance			
Closing cash balance			

Task 6

(a) Given below are the budgeted and actual cash flows for a catering company for the month of December 20X5.

Complete the table below to calculate each variance between actual and budget and state whether it is favourable or adverse.

	Actual £	Budget £	Variance £	Fav/Adv £
Sales receipts	154,000	175,000		
Food costs	−72,500	−64,000		
Salaries	−43,000	−43,000		
Administrative costs	−25,400	−27,600		
Capital expenditure	−64,000	−18,000		
Dividend	−20,000	0		
Deposit account interest	100	100		
Net cash flow	−70,800	22,500		
Opening cash balance	31,400	30,000		
Closing cash balance	−39,400	52,500		

(b) **Suggest a possible cause for the** Sales receipts, Materials costs, Administrative costs, Capital expenditure and Dividend **variances and suggest four actions which could have reduced the overdraft**.

Task 7

(a) **Which of the following describes the cash operating cycle?**

Inventory – receivables + cash ☐

Receivables– payables + inventory + cash ☐

Cash + inventory – payables ☐

Receivables + inventory + cash + payables ☐

(b) **Selecting from the picklists complete the following sentences.**

Over-trading occurs when a business has [too much/too little] working capital.
Over-capitalisation occurs when a business has [too much/too little] working capital.

(c) **XYZ Ltd is able to exactly match its trade payables payment period with its trade receivables collection period. As a result its cash operating cycle depends purely on its inventory holding policy.**

True ☐

False ☐

(d) Extracts from the financial statements of QWE Co for the years ended 31 March are as follows.

	20X6 £'000	20X7 £'000
Inventories	240	265
Purchases of raw materials	600	850
Cost of sales	1,570	1,830
Administrative expenses	45	65
Sales	1,684	1,996
Trade receivables	114	200
Trade payables	50	70
Overdraft	400	950
Additions to non-current assets	700	900

Cost of sales includes all relevant production costs including manufacturing overheads and labour.

Calculate the length in days of the company's operating cycle for the year ended 31 March 20X7. ☐

....

Task 8

(a) **What are the advantages of each type of financing In the table below?**

Type of finance	Advantages
Bank loan	
Overdraft	

(b) The directors of FH Panels Ltd have identified the opportunity to purchase a freehold property at a cost of £1,100,000. They will also require additional working capital for the project of £100,000.

What would normally be the best method of financing these two elements of the project?

Freehold property	Working capital	
Overdraft	Overdraft	☐
Bank loan	Bank loan	☐
Bank loan	Overdraft	☐
Overdraft	Bank loan	☐

(c) **Complete the table to below to indicate the effect that certain actions by a company would have on any overdraft finance.**

	Increase overdraft (tick)	Decrease overdraft (tick)
Increase inventory levels		
Improve credit control procedures		
Increase quantity of sales		
Drawings taken by the owner		

Task 9

Discuss the dangers to a company of a high level of gearing, including in your answer an explanation of the following terms:

(i)   Business risk
(ii) Financial risk

· ·

Task 10

A company has an investment policy which specifies the following:

· Investments must be medium-low risk.
· The maximum to be invested in a single investment is £50,000.
· The minimum required return is 3% p.a.
· An investment must be convertible into cash within 1 month.

The company has £100,000 to invest and is considering the following options:

Option 1:

Minimum investment £60,000, interest rate 3.9% p.a., 30 day notice period, the majority of the investment is held in Treasury stock, with a small amount in shares of FTSE100 quoted companies.

Option 2:

No minimum investment, interest rate 3% p.a., investment in Gilts.

Option 3:

Minimum investment £50,000; bank deposit account, interest rate 3.5% p.a., 30 day notice period.

Option 4:

No minimum investment, investment in portfolio of shares in quoted companies, interest rate 4.5% p.a., no notice period

(a) **Assess whether the investment options comply with the company's investment policy and recommend an appropriate investment strategy for the company, showing the investments in order of preference**

(b) **Explain the role of financial intermediaries and how they can reduce risk for investors.**

BPP PRACTICE ASSESSMENT 2
CASH MANAGEMENT

ANSWERS

Task 1

	£
Receipts for sales	163,000
Payments for purchases	74,000
Factory rent paid	32,000
Administrative expenses paid	13,000
Delivery lorry expenses paid	14,000
Depreciation	0

Workings

Receipts for sales	=	170,000 + 32,000 − 39,000	=	163,000
Payments for purchases	=	72,000 + 17,000 − 15,000	=	74,000
Factory rent paid	=	31,000 − 6,000 + 7,000	=	32,000
Administrative expenses	=	14,000 + 1,000 − 2,000	=	13,000
Lorry expenses	=	16,000 + 2,000 − 4,000	=	14,000
Depreciation	=	0 (this is not a cash expense)		

Task 2

(a)

	Production volume Units	Trend Units	Monthly variation (volume less trend) Units
January	90,000		
February	98,000	100,000	−2,000
March	112,000	102,000	+10,000
April	96,000	104,000	−8,000
May	104,000	106,000	−2,000
June	118,000	108,000	+10,000
July	102,000	110,000	−8,000
August	110,000	112,000	−2,000
September	124,000	114,000	+10,000
October	108,000	116,000	−8,000
November	116,000	118,000	−2,000
December	130,000		

The monthly sales volume trend is $\boxed{2,000}$ units.

(This is calculated as (£118,000 – £100,000)/9 interval gaps).

(b)

	Forecast trend Units	Variation Units	Forecast sales volume Units
January (118,000 + (2 × 2000))	122,000	–8,000	114,000
February (118,000 + (3 × 2,000)	124,000	–2,000	122,000
March (118,000 + (4 × 3,000))	126,000	+10,000	136,000

Task 3

	Workings	January £	February £	March £
Cash sales			800	800
Opening receivables		125,000	35,000	
January sales	104,000 × 40%	41,600		
	104,000 × 50%		52,000	
	104,000 × 10%			10,400
February sales	140,000 × 40%		56,000	
	140,000 × 50%			70,000
March sales	155,000 × 40%			62,000
Total receipts from sales		**166,600**	**143,800**	**143,200**

Task 4

(a)

	Workings	January £	February £	March £
Total sales		104,000	140,800	155,800
Cost of sales	104,000 × 0.6	62,400		
	140,800 × 0.6		84,480	
	155,800 × 0.6			93,480
Split:				
Ingredients	62,400 × 0.3	18,720		
	84,480 × 0.3		25,344	
	93,480 × 0.3			28,044
Labour and overheads	62,400 × 0.7	43,680		
	84,480 × 0.7		59,136	
	93,480 × 0.7			65,436

(b)

	January £	February £	March £	Trade payables at 31 March £
Payment to suppliers	17,600	18,720	25,344	28,044
Payment for labour and overheads	43,680	59,136	65,436	
Total cash payments	61,280	77,856	90,780	

Task 5

	January £	February £	March £
Cash receipts			
Receipts from sales	153,400	148,800	145,600
Deposit account interest	100	100	100
Total cash receipts	**153,500**	**148,900**	**145,700**
Cash payments			
Payments to suppliers	−70,000	−41,600	−56,000
Salaries	−43,000	−43,000	−45,150
Administration overheads	−27,000	−30,000	−30,000
Capital expenditure		−20,000	−6,000
Total payments	**−140,000**	**−134,600**	**−137,150**
Net cash flow	**13,500**	**14,300**	**8,550**
Opening cash balance	−39,400	−25,900	−11,600
Closing cash balance	**−25,900**	**−11,600**	**−3,050**

Task 6

(a)

	Actual £	Budget £	Variance £	Fav/Adv £
Sales receipts	154,000	175,000	21,000	Adv
Food costs	−72,500	−64,000	8,500	Adv
Salaries	−43,000	−43,000	0	
Administrative costs	−25,400	−27,600	2,200	Fav
Capital expenditure	−64,000	−18,000	46,000	Adv
Dividend	−20,000	0	20,000	Adv
Deposit account interest	100	100	0	
Net cash flow	−70,800	22,500	93,300	Adv
Opening cash balance	31,400	30,000	1,400	Fav
Closing cash balance	−39,400	52,500	91,900	Adv

(b)

Sales receipts	Loss of customers
Materials costs	Increase in suppliers prices
Administrative costs	Cost cutting
Capital expenditure	Unplanned expenditure
Dividend	Unplanned discretionary payment

Actions to reduce overdraft	Delayed payments to suppliers
	Delayed capital expenditure
	Delayed dividend
	Took out a bank loan for capital expenditure

Task 7

(a) Receivables – payables + inventory + cash

(b) Over-trading occurs when a business has <u>too little</u> working capital.

Over-capitalisation occurs when a business has <u>too much</u> working capital.

(c) True

(d) **Length of operating cycle** = 365 × (average raw materials/Purchases + Average finished goods/Cost of sales + Average receivables/Sales + Average payables/Purchases)

= 365 × (0.5(55 + 80)/850 + 185/1,830 + 05(114 + 200)/1,996 – 0.5(50 +70)/850)
= 29.0 days + 36.9 days + 28.7 days – 25.8 days
= 68.8 days

Task 8

(a)

Type of finance	Advantages
Bank loan	Relatively low cost
	Repayments can be negotiated
Overdraft	Security not normally required
	Useful to fund working capital
	Precise amount required does not need to be known
	Covenants not normally included

(b)   The correct answer is

Freehold property   **Working capital**

Bank loan   Overdraft

(c)

	Increase overdraft (tick)	Decrease overdraft (tick)
Increase inventory levels	✓	
Improve credit control procedures		✓
Increase quantity of sales		✓
Drawings taken by the owner	✓	

Task 9

(i)   **Business risk**, the inherent risk of doing business for a company, refers to the risk of making only low profits, or even losses, due to the nature of the business that the company is involved in. A business which requires a high level of fixed costs and has a relatively low or volatile pattern of income or cash inflows may have trouble covering its payables including interest payments on debt, and so the level of business risk will be high. If fixed costs are low, and fairly easily covered, the business risk, in this aspect, will be low.

(ii)   A high level of debt creates **financial risk**. This is the risk of a company not being able to meet other obligations as a result of the need to make interest payments. The proportion of debt finance carried by a company is therefore as significant as the level of business risk. Financial risk can be seen from different points of view.

(1) **The company** as a whole. If a company's gearing ratio increases it may struggle to service the debt that it already has and will have difficulty raising new debt finance. If the company builds up debts that it cannot pay when they fall due, it will be forced into liquidation.

(2) **Lenders to the company**. From the lender's viewpoint, the interest rate charged on loan finance will normally reflect the risk associated with the loan and an assessment of a company's creditworthiness will be made. If a company cannot pay its debts, the company will go into liquidation owing its creditors money that they are unlikely to recover in full. This is particularly true in relation to unsecured loans and trade payables.

(3) **Ordinary shareholders**. A company will not make any dividend payments unless it is able to earn enough profit before interest and tax to pay all its interest charges, and then tax. The lower the profits or the higher the interest-bearing debts, the less there will be, if there is anything at all, for shareholders. This greater financial risk should be reflected in shareholders demanding a higher risk premium and therefore a higher cost of capital for the company.

Task 10

(a) Compliance with investment policy

	Risk high/med/low	Within company's maximum investment limit Yes/No	Annual Return %	Liquidity acceptable (1 month conversion) Yes/No?
Option 1	Medium	No	3.9%	Yes
Option 2	Low	Yes	3%	Yes
Option 3	Low	Yes	3.5%	Yes
Option 4	High	Yes	4.5%	Yes

Note: As Gilts are readily marketable securities they should be convertible into cash within 1 month.

All of the investment options have an acceptable level of liquidity, as they are all convertible to cash within 1 month. They also all satisfy the minimum return required of 3%.

Option 1 would be rejected for having too high a minimum investment value, and option 4 has a high level of risk.

Therefore the acceptable investments are options 2 and 3.

BPP LEARNING MEDIA

Investment strategy

Given the maximum investment requirement, the investment should be split between the options. The return from option 3 is higher than the return from option 2, therefore the recommended investment strategy is:

	Recommended Option (insert number)	Amount invested £	Total return £
Preferred Option	3	50,000	1,750
Next best Option	2	50,000	1,500
Total		100,000	3,250

Overall the company will earn a 3.25% return on its investment.

Working: 3,250/100,000 = 3.25%

(b) **Role of financial intermediaries**

Financial intermediaries provide a link between investors who have surplus cash and borrowers who have a need for finance.

Financial intermediaries aggregate invested funds. This means that they group together the small amounts of cash provided by individual investors, so that borrowers who need large amounts of cash have a convenient and readily accessible route to obtain necessary funds.

Risk reduction

Financial intermediaries reduce the risk for individual lenders by pooling. They will assume the risk of loss on short-term funds borrowed by business organisations. Such losses are shared among lenders in general.

Financial intermediaries also bridge the gap between the wish of most lenders (investors) for liquidity and the desire of most borrowers for loans over longer periods.

BPP PRACTICE ASSESSMENT 3
CASH MANAGEMENT

Time allowed: 2.5 hours

Task 1

The cash budget for Speights Ltd for the three months ended June has been partially completed. The following information is to be incorporated and the cash budget completed.

- Fixed production overheads are £25,000 per month. This includes depreciation of £5,000.
- Sales department costs are expected to be fixed at £12,000 per month including depreciation of £500 per month.
- The costs for the Speights Ltd's retail shop are fixed and are £7,000 per month including depreciation of £800.
- Administration overheads should be budgeted to be £25,000 each month.
- Overdraft interest is charged by the bank each month and should be budgeted at the rate of 1% per month on the overdrawn balance at the end of the previous month.
- All of the above costs are paid for in the month that they were incurred.

Using the additional information above, complete the cash budget for Speights Ltd for the three months ending in June. Cash inflows should be entered as positive figures and cash outflows as negative figures. Zeroes must be entered where appropriate to achieve full marks.

	April £	May £	June £
Receipts			
Total receipts – sales receipts	205,000	222,600	225,885
Payments			
Payments to suppliers	–110,000	–66,000	–86,000
Payments for wages	–62,000	–57,500	–72,000
Fixed production overhead			
Sales department costs			
Shop costs			
Administration overheads			
Overdraft interest			
Total payments			
Net cash flow			
Bank balance b/f	–220,000		
Bank balance c/f			

Task 2

(a) Lucent Ltd has been carrying out time series analysis on its sales volumes for the last three years. It wishes to use this time series analysis to forecast sales volumes for one of its shops which sells speciality products, for April, May and June 20X6.

The trend has been discovered to be a monthly increase of 20 units. In March 20X6 the trend figure for sales volume was 2,040 units. The time series analysis has also identified the following seasonal variations for months involved:

April	+43 units
May	+10 units
June	−25 units

The selling price of each unit is £12.

Monthly purchases are on average 60% of the value of sales.

Using the trend and monthly variations complete the table below to forecast the sales volume, sales value and purchases value for April, May and June 20X6.

	Forecast trend	Variation	Forecast sales volume	Forecast sales £	Forecast purchases £
April					
May					
June					

Additional information

As well as time series analysis the business wants to forecast wages costs for the shop each period using an industry average wage rate index. The wages cost in March 20X6 was £10,200 when the wage rate index stood at 121. The forecast wage rate index for the next three months is as follows:

April	125
May	130
June	137

(b) **What will be the forecast wages cost for each of the months of April, May and June 20X6?**

Month	Wages cost £
April	
May	
June	

Task 3

A candle making company is preparing its cash budget for the three months ending June 20X6.

Production is expected to be 130,000 candles in April, 135,000 candles in May and 140,000 candles in June.

There is one unit of raw materials for each candle and there are currently 100,000 units of raw materials in the warehouse and it is intended to maintain inventory at this level.

The cost of raw materials for each candle is 60 pence. No price increase is expected in the budgetary period. All purchases are made in the month of production but not paid for until the following month. At 31 March 20X6 the payable for purchases made during March was £120,000.

(a) **Complete the table below to determine the raw materials purchases budget in both units and £ for each of the three months ending in June.**

	Workings	April Units	May Units	June Units
Production				
Opening inventory				
Closing inventory				
Purchases in units				
		£	£	£
Purchases in £				

(b) **Complete the table below to show the payments to suppliers for each of the three months ending in June.**

	Workings	April £	May £	June £
Opening payables				
April purchases				
May purchases				

Task 4

The cash budget for Magic Ltd for the three months ended December 20X1 has been partially completed. The following information is to be incorporated and the cash budget completed.

Additional information

- Capital expenditure of £24,000 should be budgeted for in October. This will give rise to additional depreciation of £200 per month which is to be included in production overheads.
- In addition to the depreciation mentioned above, production overheads are expected to be £14,000 per month.
- Repairs and maintenance costs should be budgeted at an average of £750 per month.
- The cash balance at 30 September 20X1 was £13,900.
- A dividend of £17,500 is due to be paid at the end of November.
- The Sales department is running a big advertising campaign in September. This is expected to cost £6,450 and will be paid for a month later.

Using the additional information above, complete the cash budget for Magic Ltd for the three months ending in December 20X1. Cash inflows should be entered as positive figures and cash outflows as negative figures. Zeroes must be entered where appropriate to achieve full marks.

Cash budget for three months ending 30 December 20X1

	October £	November £	December £
Receipts:			
Receipts from customers	+89,400	+102,300	+93,600
Payments:			
Payments to suppliers	−37,500	−45,600	−33,500
Wages	−22,000	−22,000	−22,000
Production overheads			
Advertising campaign			
Repairs and maintenance			
Capital expenditure			
Dividend			
Total payments:			
Net cash flow			
Opening cash balance			
Closing cash balance			

Task 5

A business has prepared the following cash budget for three months ending 30 September 20X6.

	July £	August £	September £
Receipts:			
Receipts from customers	104,697	106,284	109,296
Payments:			
Payments to suppliers	−50,200	−52,600	−51,400
Wages	−21,300	−21,900	−23,700
Production overheads	−10,000	−10,500	−10,500
Selling overheads	−3,200	−3,200	−3,200
Repairs and maintenance	−2,500	−2,500	−2,500
Capital expenditure	0	−20,000	0
Total payments:	−87,200	−110,700	−91,300
Net cash flow	17,497	−4,416	17,996
Opening cash balance	23,900	41,397	36,981
Closing cash balance	41,397	36,981	54,977

The following additional information has now come to light:

1. Suppliers are currently paid one month after the date of purchase (so the budgeted payment of £50,200 in July relates to June's purchases). To reduce material costs, from 1 July 20X6 the business intends to take advantage of a 5% discount by settling supplier invoices in the month of purchase. September purchases are expected to be £54,000.

2. Since preparing the budget the business has agreed to give the workers a 3% pay rise with effect from 1 August. Wages are paid in the month incurred.

3. A payment for advertising of £2,000 has been omitted from September's selling overheads.

4. Capital expenditure relates to a machine. The £500 increase in production overheads from August relates to depreciation on the new machine.

5. Interest is to be charged monthly, at a rate of 1%, on any overdraft at the start of the month.

Using the additional information above, complete the table below to show the revised cash budget for the three months ending September. Cash inflows should be entered as positive figures and cash outflows as negative figures. Zeroes must be entered where appropriate to achieve full marks.

	July £	August £	September £
Receipts:			
Receipts from customers	104,697	106,284	109,296
Payments:			
Payments to suppliers			
Wages			
Production overheads			
Selling overheads			
Repairs and maintenance	–2,500	–2,500	–2,500
Capital expenditure	0	–20,000	0
Interest on overdraft			
Total payments:			
Net cash flow			
Opening cash balance	23,900		
Closing cash balance			

Task 6

(a) The quarterly budget and actual figures for an organisation are provided below:

	Budgeted £	Actual £
Cash sales	22,500	28,600
Receipts from credit customers	104,000	98,760
Cash purchases	(10,800)	(7,400)
Payments to credit suppliers	(54,700)	(61,200)
Wages and salaries	(25,600)	(30,200)
General expenses	(24,600)	(20,300)
Capital expenditure	0	(20,000)
Net cash flows	10,800	(11,740)
Opening balance	2,500	2,500
Closing balance	13,300	(9,240)

Prepare a reconciliation of budgeted cash flow with actual cash flow for the quarter. Highlight the appropriate description for each entry. Use brackets to indicate figures which need to be subtracted in the reconciliation.

	£
Budgeted closing cash balance	
Surplus/shortfall in cash sales	
Surplus/shortfall in receipts from credit customers	
Increase/decrease in cash payments	
Increase/decrease in payments to credit suppliers	
Increase/decrease in wages and salaries	
Increase/decrease in general expenses	
Increase/decrease in capital expenditure	
Actual cash balance	

(b) **Suggest a possible cause for the differences between budget and actual cash sales, receipts from credit customers, payments to credit suppliers, capital expenditure**, and where appropriate **suggest a possible course of action to control these variances.**

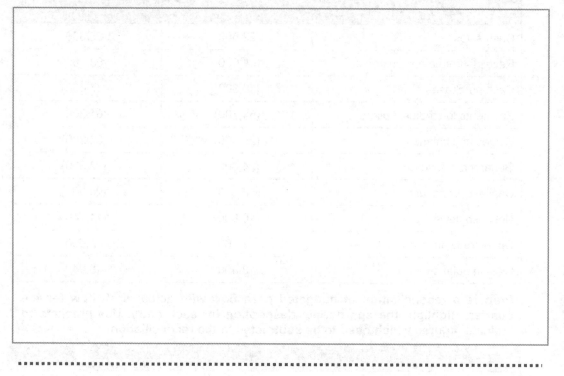

Task 7

The following financial information relates to PNP Co for the year just ended:

	£'000
Turnover	5,242.0
Variable cost of sales	3,145.0
Inventory	603.0
Receivables	744.5
Payables	574.5

Segmental analysis of receivables

	Balance	Average payment period	Discount	Bad debts
	£			£
Class 1	200,000	30 days	1.0%	none
Class 2	252,000	60 days	nil	12,600
Class 3	110,000	75 days	nil	11,000
Class 4	182,500	90 days	nil	21,900
	744,500			45,500

The receivable balances given are before taking account of irecoverable debts. All sales are on credit. Production and sales take place evenly throughout the year. Current sales for each class of receivables are in proportion to their relative year-end balances before bad debts.

It has been proposed that the discount for early payment be increased from 1.0% to 1.5% for settlement within 30 days. It is expected that this will lead to 50% of existing Class 2 receivables becoming Class 1 receivables, as well as attracting new business worth £500,000 in turnover. The new business would be divided equally between Class 1 and Class 2 receivables. Fixed costs would not increase as a result of introducing the discount or by attracting new business. PNP finances receivables from an overdraft at an annual interest rate of 8%.

Calculate the current cash operating cycle

£ [   ]

and the revised cash operating cycle caused by increasing the discount for early payment.

£ [   ]

Task 8

A business is considering an expansion project and has been looking into financing options for this project. One option is a bank loan of £400,000 with an initial facility fee of 0.5% of the loan amount and annual interest fixed at 6.5% p.a. on the original loan principal. In order to fund the working capital required for the expansion the bank has also agreed an overdraft facility of £50,000 with an annual interest rate of 11%. The owners of the business believe that the average amount of the overdraft facility that will be used is £30,000 and this will only be for the last six months of the year.

(a) **Complete the table to show the total cost of this financing arrangement for the first year.**

	Working	£
Facility fee		
Interest on loan		
Overdraft interest		
Total		

(b) Assume the loan is to be taken out for a 4 year period and that the capital plus interest will be repaid in three equal annual instalments.

Complete the table to show the total interest cost over the life of the loan and the annual repayments split between interest and capital. Work to the nearest £.

	Working	£
Total loan interest		
Total repayment (capital plus interest)		
Annual repayment		
Of which: Capital element		
Interest element		

(c) **Select from the picklists to complete the sentences below:**

The longer the period you wish to invest surplus cash for, the (1) [_____] ▼ the available interest rate is likely to be. Gilts are more suitable for (2) [_____] ▼ investments and the interest rate on them is usually (3) [_____] ▼ . Treasury Bills, issued by the (4) [_____] ▼ are (5) [_____] ▼ investments which (6) [_____] ▼ be traded. Gilts and Treasury stock are considered to be (7) [_____] ▼ investments and as a result will offer a (8) [_____] ▼ rate of return than an investment in equity shares.

Picklist:

Higher/lower
Short term/long term
Fixed/variable
Stock exchange/government/local authority
Short term/long term
Can/cannot
High risk/low risk
Higher/lower

(d) An investment of £500,000 is made in a money market account which pays interest of 2.8% per annum.

How much interest will be received if the investment is held for 3 months?

£ [_____]

(e)   A company purchases gilts with a nominal value of £100,000 for a price of £94,000.

On maturity the company will receive £94,000.

Is this statement true or false?

True   ☐

False   ☐

....

Task 9

(a)   **Explain the difference between an overdraft and a loan and the circumstances when each might be used.**

(b) A company has an aggressive approach to working capital management, whereby all fluctuating assets (assets held over and above the minimum amounts) plus a certain proportion of permanent current assets are financed by short-term capital such as bank overdrafts and trade payables.

What could be the problems of this approach and what alternative financing sources could the company consider?

Task 10

A company has forecast that it has £50,000 available to invest for six months before the capital will be required to construct a new factory.

It is considering the following three options:

Option 1:

Invest in a mixed portfolio of shares and treasury stock. The minimum period of investment is 6 months; interest rate is 6% p.a.

Option 2:

Invest in a certificate of deposit with a six month term; interest rate is 4.5% p.a.

Option 3:

Investment in a deposit account; interest rate is 5% p.a. There is a penalty of 0.5% of capital invested for withdrawal before 12 months.

Draft an email to the financial director of the company assessing the investment options and recommending a course of action.

BPP PRACTICE ASSESSMENT 3
CASH MANAGEMENT

ANSWERS

Task 1

Cash budget for the three months ended 30 June 20X6

	April £	May £	June £
Receipts			
Total receipts – sales receipts	205,000	222,600	225,885
Payments			
Payments to suppliers	−110,000	−66,000	−86,000
Payments for wages	−62,000	−57,500	−72,000
Fixed production overhead	−20,000	−20,000	−20,000
Sales department costs	−11,500	−11,500	−11,500
Shop costs	−6,200	−6,200	−6,200
Administration overheads	−25,000	−25,000	−25,000
Overdraft interest	−2,200	−2,519	−2,180
Total payments	**−236,900**	**−188,719**	**−222,880**
Net cash flow	**−31,900**	**33,881**	**3,005**
Bank balance b/f	**−220,000**	**−251,900**	**−218,019**
Bank balance c/f	**−251,900**	**−218,019**	**−215,014**

Task 2

(a)

	Forecast trend	Variation	Forecast sales volume	Forecast sales £	Forecast purchases £
April	2,060	+43	2,103	25,236	15,142
May	2,080	+10	2,090	25,080	15,048
June	2,100	−25	2,075	24,900	14,940

(b)

Month	Wages cost £
April 10,200 × 125/121	10,537
May 10,200 × 130/121	10,959
June 10,200 × 137/121	11,549

Task 3

(a) Purchases budget

	Workings	April Units	May Units	June Units
Production		130,000	135,000	140,000
Opening inventory		−100,000	−100,000	−100,000
Closing inventory		100,000	100,000	100,000
Purchases in units		**130,000**	**135,000**	**140,000**
		£	£	£
Purchases in £ (units × £0.60)		**78,000**	**81,000**	**84,000**

(b) Payments to suppliers

	Workings	April £	May £	June £
Opening payables		120,000		
April purchases			78,000	
May purchases				81,000

Task 4

Cash budget for three months ending 30 December 20X1

	October £	November £	December £
Receipts:			
Receipts from customers	**+89,400**	**+102,300**	**+93,600**
Payments:			
Payments to suppliers	−37,500	−45,600	−33,500
Wages	−22,000	−22,000	−22,000
Production overheads	−14,000	−14,000	−14,000
Advertising campaign	−6,450		
Repairs and maintenance	−750	−750	−750
Capital expenditure	−24,000		
Dividend		−17,500	
Total payments:	**−104,700**	**−99,850**	**70,250**
Net cash flow	−15,300	+2,450	+23,350
Opening cash balance	+13,900	−1,400	+1,050
Closing cash balance	−1,400	+1,050	+24,400

Task 5

	July £	August £	September £
Receipts:			
Receipts from customers	104,697	106,284	109,296
Payments:			
Payments to suppliers			
June purchases (1 month credit)	−50,200		
July purchases (52,600 × 0.95)	−49,970		
August purchases (51,400 × 0.95)		−48,830	
September purchases (54,000 × 0.95)			−51,300
Wages			
21,300	−21,300		
21,900 × 1.03		−22,557	
23,700 × 1.03			−24,411
Production overheads	−10,000	−10,000	−10,000
Selling overheads	−3,200	−3,200	−5,200
Repairs and maintenance	−2,500	−2,500	−2,500
Capital expenditure	0	−20,000	0
Interest on overdraft	0	−86	−95
Total payments:	−137,170	−107,173	−93,506
Net cash flow	−32,473	−889	15,790
Opening cash balance	23,900	−8,573	−9,462
Closing cash balance	−8,573	−9,462	6,328

Task 6

(a)

	£
Budgeted closing cash balance	13,300
Surplus in cash sales	6,100
Shortfall in receipts from credit customers	−5,240
Decrease in cash payments	3,400
Increase in payments to credit suppliers	−6,500
Increase in wages and salaries	−4,600
Decrease in general expenses	4,300
Increase in capital expenditure	−20,000
Actual cash balance	**−9,240**

(b)

Surplus of cash sales	Higher overall sales, or a lower price (settlement discount) offered for immediate receipt of cash.
	This is a beneficial variance, so the company may seek to enhance these rather than control them, however, if a discount is being offered for cash payment, care should be taken to ensure that the values of the discount compared to the cost of financing the credit term is financially worthwhile.
Shortfall in receipts from credit customers	This could be caused by sales being made for cash rather than on credit, customers taking longer to pay, or a key customer goes into liquidation.
	Longer payment periods can be managed by improving credit control, and while customer liquidations are outside the control of the company to a certain extent, the continued monitoring of customers creditworthiness can indicate problems in advance and steps could be taken to limit or stop the credit offered.

Increase in payments to credit suppliers	Payments to suppliers being made earlier, bulk buying arrangements or unexpected increase in production requirements.
	Whether or not this is a problem depends on the reasons for this taking place – if payments are being made early to take advantage of beneficial early payment or bulk discounts, then these are worthwhile. If however the payments are simply taking place earlier than required, this could be damaging to the liquidity needs of the company and should be curtailed.
Increase in capital expenditure	Unexpected breakdown of necessary machinery which cannot be repaired or capital expenditure which has not been budgeted for is being incurred.
	Improve budgeting procedures would control the unbudgeted expenditure issue.

Task 7

Current cash operating cycle: 55 days

Inventory days = 603/3,145 × 365 = 70 days
Payables days = 574.5/3,145 × 365 = 67 days
Receivables days = 744.5/5,242 × 365 = 52 days
Cash operating cycle = 70 + 52 – 67 = 55 days

Revised cash operating cycle: 54 days

Following the implementation of the increased discount for early payment, total receivables will increase by £61,644 to £806,144 and turnover will have increased to £5,742,000. This results in a slight fall in receivable days to 51 days (806,144/5,742,000 × 365) and therefore a slight fall of one day in the cash operating cycle to 54 days.

Workings

Total receivables increase

£250,000/(365/30) = £20,548

£250,000/(365/60) = £41,096

Turnover

£5,242,000 + £500,000 = £5,742,000

Task 8

(a)

	Working	£
Facility fee	0.5% × £400,000	2,000
Interest on loan	6.5% × £400,000	26,000
Overdraft interest	11% × 30,000 × 6/12	1,650
Total		29,650

(b)

	Working	£
Total loan interest	6.5% × 400,000 × 4	104,000
Total repayment (capital plus interest)	400,000 + 104,000	504,000
Annual repayment	504,000/3	168,000
Of which: Capital element	400,000/3	133,333
Interest element	104,000/3	34,667

(c) The longer the period you wish to invest surplus cash for, the (1) higher the available interest rate is likely to be. Gilts are more suitable for (2) long term investments and the interest rate on them is usually (3) fixed . Treasury Bills, issued by the (4) government are (5) short term investments which (6) can be traded. Gilts and Treasury stock are considered to be (7) low risk investments and as a result will offer a (8) lower rate of return than an investment in equity shares.

(d) £500,000 × 2.8% × 3/12 = £3,500

(e) False. The company will receive the nominal value of £100,000.

Task 9

(a) An overdraft will tend to have a higher rate of interest than a bank loan. The interest will be charged on the amount of the facility used. An overdraft is repayable on demand and is particularly useful for funding working capital or for short-term finance requirements eg due to seasonality.

A bank loan will be for a fixed term and interest will be charged on the whole amount, regardless of how much of the funds are used. A loan may have covenants attached to it by the lender. In addition the lender may require security in the form of a charge on the assets of the business. There are two types of charge which could be required, a floating charge is a charge on the current assets of the company – the company can buy and sell the assets on which the floating charge is secured. A fixed charge is a charge on a specific asset and the company is not permitted to sell the asset without discharging the debt beforehand.

A loan would normally be used for the purchase of non-current assets. The term of the bank loan should be matched with the life of the assets that it finances, so that the income generated can be used for debt servicing.

(b) Aggressive management

Current assets can be broken down into two portions, *permanent* current assets and *fluctuating* current assets. The permanent current assets represent base levels of inventories, receivables, etc., that will always be on hand. Fluctuating current assets represent the seasonal build-ups that occur, such as inventories before Christmas and receivables after Christmas.

There is no problem financing fluctuating current assets with short-term finance as a business does not want to pay financing charges all year if it only needs the money for a short period.

The permanent current assets are, individually, short life assets, but they represent minimum balances that will always need to be financed. While it is possible to finance permanent working capital needs with short-term debt, it is risky to do so:

Short-term interest rates fluctuate much more than long-term interest rates. Also if the company has a bad year it may find that lenders are unwilling to continue to extend the overdraft.

Thus aggressive management will mean that there is an increased risk of cash flow and liquidity problems.

Businesses may also suffer higher interest costs on short-term sources of finance.

Alternative financing

It is less risky if permanent current assets are financed long-term, like non-current assets.

If short-term methods cannot be used, long-term funding such as long-term loans or share capital not tied up in funding non-current assets will be used to support working capital. This will mean that working capital is managed conservatively, with all non-current assets and permanent current assets, as well as part of fluctuating current assets, being financed by long-term capital. When fluctuating current assets are low, there will be surplus cash which the company will be able to invest in marketable securities.

Task 10

Email

To: fd@company.co.uk   **Date**:   Today

From: aatstudent@company.co.uk   **Subject**:   Investment options

The company has £50,000 to invest for a period of six months. As the investment is required for the construction of the factory, it is important

that we do not expose the company to capital risk.

If the company selects Option 1, the total return on the investment will be £1,500.

If the company selects Option 2, the total return on the investment will be £1,125.

If the company selects Option 3, the total return on the investment will be £1,000.

I recommend that Option 2 be selected as this will have the lowest risk for the company. The investment will earn a return, after six months, of 2.25 %.

Workings:

Option 1: £50,000 × 6% × 6/12 = £1,500

Option 2: £50,000 × 4.5% × 6/12 = £1,125

Option 3: £50,000 × 5% × 6/12 = £1,250 less penalty for early withdrawal £250 (0.5% × £50,000) = £1,000

BPP PRACTICE ASSESSMENT 4
CASH MANAGEMENT

Time allowed: 2.5 hours

PRACTICE ASSESSMENT 4

Task 1

(a) **Complete the table from the lists below by filling in a description of the type of payment and suggesting three transactions for each type of payment.**

Type of payment	Description	Example transactions
Discretionary		
Non-discretionary		

(b) The statement of profit or loss of a business for the three months ended 31 December shows that there is sales revenue of £175,000.

Extracts from the sales ledger control account at 1 October and 31 December show the following balances:

	31 December	1 October
Trade receivables	£60,500	£64,000

Drag and drop the entries to the correct position to complete the sales ledger control account then enter the correct figure for the cash received from customers in the period:

Balance b/d
Balance c/d
Sales
60,500
64,000
175,000

Sales ledger control account			
	Dr £		Cr £
		Cash received (balancing figure) _____	_____
	_____		_____

Task 2

(a) You are given an extract from a company's records about the average hourly wage rate.

Complete the table to show the wage rate index for each month.

	Actual hourly wage rate	Wage rate Index
January	£6.00	100
February	£6.36	
March	£6.48	
April	£6.72	
May	£6.72	
June	£6.84	

(b) Each unit of product requires 3 hours of labour and the production budget for July is to manufacture 12,500 units.

If the index for July is 115 what is the budgeted payment for labour hours?

Payment for July labour hours

£ [   ]

The trend figures for sales in £ for a business for the four quarters of last year and the seasonal variations are estimated as:

	Trend sales £	Seasonal variations
Quarter 1	160,000	+12,820
Quarter 2	164,500	+14,805
Quarter 3	169,000	-5,070
Quarter 4	173,500	-22,555

(c) **Assuming the trend continues, complete the table to show the forecast sales for each of the four quarters of next year.**

	This year's trend sales £	Additive adjustment for seasonal variation	Sales budget
Quarter 1			
Quarter 2			
Quarter 3			
Quarter 4			

(d) The overhead costs of a company have been found to be accurately represented by the formula

$y = £10,000 + £0·25x$

where y is the monthly cost and x represents the activity level measured as the number of orders.

Monthly activity levels of orders may be estimated using a combined regression analysis and time series model:

$a = 100,000 + 30b$

where a represents the de-seasonalised monthly activity level and b represents the month number.

In month 240, the seasonal index value is 108.

Calculate the overhead cost for month 240 to the nearest £1,000.

....

Task 3

A business buys handbags from a wholesaler and then sells them to customers, in the same month, at a mark-up of 60% on cost.

30% of the sales are cash and 70% are on credit. 80% of credit customers pay one month later and the remaining 20% pay 2 months after the date of sale.

Complete the tables below to show the total sales for the three months from October to December, the split between cash and credit sales, the timing of cash receipts and the trade receivables at the end of December. Round to whole £'s throughout and enter zeroes where appropriate.

	October £	November £	December £
Purchases of handbags	120,000	130,000	140,000
Total sales			
Split:			
Cash sales			
Credit sales			

	Working	Oct cash received £	Nov cash received £	Dec cash received £	y/e trade receivables £
Cash sales					
Cash from credit sales:					
October					
October					
November					
November					
December					
Total					

Task 4

Property Co has been in business for only a short time and is preparing a cash budget for the first four months of 20X6. Expected sales are as follows.

Month	20X5 December	20X6 January	20X6 February	20X6 March	20X6 April
Units sold	10	10	15	25	30

The average price of each unit is £5,400 and Property Co receives 1/3 of its income in the month of sale and the remaining 2/3 in the month after sale. The company has nine employees who are paid on a monthly basis. The average salary per employee is £35,000 per year. If more than 20 units are sold in a given month, each employee is paid in that month a bonus of £140 for each additional unit sold.

Variable expenses are incurred at the rate of 16.67% of the value of each unit sold and these expenses are paid in the month of sale. Fixed overheads of £4,300 per month are paid in the month in which they arise. The company pays interest every three months on a loan of £200,000 at a simple interest rate of 6% per year. The last interest payment in each year is paid in December.

An outstanding tax liability of £95,800 is due to be paid in April. In the same month the company intends to dispose of surplus vehicles, with a carrying value of £15,000, for £20,000. The cash balance at the start of January 20X6 is expected to be a deficit of £40,000.

Prepare a monthly cash budget for the period from January to April 20X6. Your budget must clearly indicate each item of income and expenditure, and the opening and closing monthly cash balances.

	Jan £'000	Feb £'000	March £'000	April £'000
Receipts				
Fee on sale				
Receipt on sale of vehicles				
Payments				
Salaries				
Bonus				
Variable expenses				
Fixed overheads				
Interest on loan				
Tax liability				
Net cash flow				
Balance b/fwd				
Balance c/fwd				

Task 5

A business needs help deciding whether or not to introduce a prompt payment discount in order to collect cash from its credit customers in sooner.

The sales budget is as follows:

	£
Period 1 sales	144,000
Period 2 sales	151,500
Period 3 sales	145,450
Period 4 sales	139,000
Period 5 sales	162,300

The original cash receipts budget was prepared assuming that 60% of sales were paid for by customers in the month following the sale and the remaining 37% of customers paid two months after the sale, with 3% of all debts remaining uncollected.

	Period 3 £	Period 4 £	Period 5 £
Period 1 sales £144,000 × 37%	53,280		
Period 2 sales £151,500 × 60%	90,900		
Period 2 sales £151,500 × 37%		56,055	
Period 3 sales £145,450 × 60%		87,270	
Period 3 sales £145,450 × 37%			53,817
Period 4 sales £139,000 × 60%			83,400
Total receipts from customers	**144,180**	**143,325**	**137,217**

The company is considering introducing a settlement discount at the start of period 3. The discount will be 2% for payments made in the month of the sale. This policy is expected to result in 40% of customers paying in the month of the sale, 30% paying in the month following the sale and the remaining 30% paying two months following the sale. As cash is being collected faster, the company is expecting to eliminate irrecoverable debts. It also expects sales to increase by 5% from period 3 because more customers will be attracted by the change in credit policy.

(a) **Complete the table below to calculate the forecast receipts from customers for each of periods 3, 4 and 5 if the system of settlement discounts is introduced.**

	Workings	Period 3 £	Period 4 £	Period 5 £
Period 1 sales				
Period 2 sales				
Period 2 sales				
Period 3 sales				
Period 3 sales				
Period 3 sales				
Period 4 sales				
Period 4 sales				
Period 5 sales				
Total receipts from customers				

(b) **Complete the tables below to show the effects of introducing the discount system.**

	Period 3 £	Period 4 £	Period 5 £
Original receipts from customers			
Revised receipts from customers			
Overall increase/(decrease) in sales receipts			

Cost of prompt payment discount	Workings	Period 3 £	Period 4 £	Period 5 £
Period 3 sales				
Period 4 sales				
Period 5 sales				

Task 6

(a) The quarterly budget and actual figures for an organisation are provided below.

Complete the table to show the variance arising and use a + or – to indicate whether it is favourable or adverse.

	Budgeted cash flows £	Actual cash flows £	Variance £
Cash sales	32,500	28,600	
Receipts from credit customers	234,000	198,760	
Sale of machinery	0	7,500	
Payments to credit suppliers	(124,700)	(91,200)	
Wages and salaries	(35,600)	(30,200)	
General expenses	(14,600)	(10,300)	
Capital expenditure	0	(20,000)	
Drawings	(30,000)	(35,000)	
Net cash flows	61,600	48,160	
Opening balance	32,500	32,500	
Closing balance	94,100	80,660	

(b) **Explain what impact the following situations might have on the cash budget.**

Some customers, who previously bought goods on credit, are taking advantage of lower prices offered on cash sales

A machine needed to be replaced unexpectedly when it broke down

Material costs have decreased

Large orders necessitated additional overtime working

Task 7

(a) **Which one of the following equations best describes the cash operating cycle?**

average inventory holding period + average trade payables' payment period
– average trade receivables' collection period ☐

average inventory holding period + average trade receivables' collection period
– average trade payables' payment period ☐

average cash balance + average trade receivables' collection period
– average trade payables' payment period ☐

average cash balance – average trade receivables' collection period
+ average trade payables' payment period ☐

(b) **Which of the following should a business do in order to improve its cash operating cycle?**

Increase inventories of raw material ☐

Decrease the credit period taken from trade suppliers ☐

Extend the credit period for customers ☐

Reduce the time taken to produce its product ☐

(c) A company's current cash operating cycle is 34 days.

Which of the following will have the effect of reducing the cash operating cycle?

Increasing the inventory holding period by 3 days ☐

Decreasing the trade payables' payment period by 5 days ☐

Decreasing the trade receivables' collection period by 2 days ☐

Increasing the average cash balance by 10% ☐

(d) A company wishes to minimise its inventory costs. Annual demand for a raw material costing £12 per unit is 60,000 units per year. Inventory management costs for this raw material are as follows:

Ordering cost: £6 per order

The supplier of this raw material has offered a bulk purchase discount of 1% for order quantities of 10,000 units or more.

Calculate the cost of inventory if the discount is taken up.

£ [   ]

Task 8

A company has forecast the balance on the business bank account at the end of each of the next 6 months. Brackets indicate overdrawn balances. The company's business is seasonal and, after June, the bank account is expected to remain in credit for the remainder of the year.

Month	£
January	3,950
February	(6,700)
March	(11,200)
April	(2,400)
May	(10,800)
June	1,250

The company has contacted the bank and has been offered the following options:

Option 1

Arrange a bank overdraft. There Is an arrangement fee of £500 to be paid in January, and interest will be charged at 12% per annum. Interest is to be calculated and charged monthly.

Option 2

Arrange a short term bank loan for the year of £12,000, with an interest rate of 8%, to be repaid in equal monthly instalments.

(a) **Complete the tables below to ascertain the cost of the two options:**

Option 1:

For the purposes of the calculation assume interest is to be charged on the forecast bank balance at the end of each month in which the overdraft is used.

Option 1	Month-end balance £	Overdraft cost £
January	3,950	
February	(6,700)	
March	(11,200)	
April	(2,400)	
May	(10,800)	
June	1,250	
Total cost		

Option 2:

Option 2	£
Total annual interest	
Monthly interest payment (Jan – Dec)	

(b) **Complete the gap fills and select from the picklists to complete the draft email to the finance director of the company :**

Email

To: [▼]   Date: Today

From: [▼]   Subject: Raising finance

The information supplied indicates that the company will have a maximum overdrawn balance of £ [▼] during the year.

If the company selects the overdraft option, the cost for the year will be £ [▼], whereas the annual cost of the short term bank loan is £ [ ].

I recommend that the [▼] option be selected as this will have the [▼] cost for the company. As the business is seasonal, the [▼] provides the [▼]. Although the interest rate on the loan is [▼], interest has to be paid for [▼] months, despite the business bank account being [▼] for more than six months of the year.

Picklist:

fd@company.co.uk	aatstudent@company.co.uk
bank overdraft	short term bank loan
highest	lowest
bank overdraft	short term bank loan
bank overdraft	short term bank loan
most flexibility	least flexibility
lower	higher
in credit	overdrawn

Task 9

In looking to reduce the working capital funding requirement, the financial controller of your company is considering factoring credit sales. The company's annual turnover is £2.5m of which 90% are credit sales. On average customers take 2.5 months to pay. Irrecoverable debts are typically 3% of credit sales. The offer from the factor is conditional on the following.

(1)   The factor will take over the sales ledger completely.

(2)   80% of the value of credit sales will be advanced immediately (as soon as sales are made to the customer), the remaining 20% will be paid to the company one month later. The factor charges 15% per annum on credit sales for advancing funds in the manner suggested. The factor is normally able to reduce the receivables' collection period to one month.

(3)   The factor offers a 'no recourse' facility whereby they take on the responsibility for dealing with irrecoverable debts. The factor is normally able to reduce irrecoverable debts to 2% of credit sales.

(4)   A charge for factoring services of 4% of credit sales will be made.

(5)   A one-off payment of £25,000 is payable to the factor.

The salary of the Receivables Ledger Administrator (£12,500) would be saved under the proposals and overhead costs of the credit control department, amounting to £2,000 per annum, would have to be reallocated. The company's cost of overdraft finance is 12% per annum.

The company pays its sales force on a commission only basis. The cost of this is 5% of credit sales and is payable immediately the sales are made. There is no intention to alter this arrangement under the factoring proposals.

Write a report to the financial controller that outlines the benefits of factoring. Include in your report an evaluation of the proposal to factor the sales ledger by comparing existing receivable collection costs with those that would result from using the factor (assuming that the factor can reduce the receivables collection period to one month).

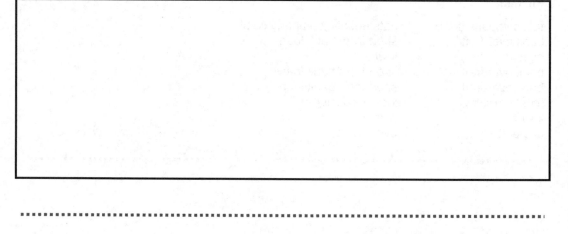

Task 10

Discuss the factors to be considered by the company when planning ways to invest any cash surplus forecast by its cash budgets.

BPP PRACTICE ASSESSMENT 4
CASH MANAGEMENT

ANSWERS

Task 1

(a)

Type of payment	Description	Example transactions
Discretionary	Payments which can validly be cancelled or delayed	Drawings Training costs Capital expenditure
Non-discretionary	Payments which must be made on time for the business to continue	PAYE and NI due to HM Revenue and Customs Payment to credit suppliers Annual loan interest

(b)

Sales ledger control account			
	Dr £		Cr £
Balance b/d	64,000		
Sales	175,000	Cash received (239,000 – 60,500)	178,500
		Balance c/d	60,500
	£239,000		£239,000

Task 2

(a)

	Actual hourly wage rate	Wage rate Index
January	£6.00	100
February	£6.36	106
March	£6.48	108
April	£6.72	112
May	£6.72	112
June	£6.84	114

(b)

Payment for July labour hours	£258,750 (12500 × 3 × £6.00 × 1.15)

(c)

	This year's trend sales £	Additive adjustment for seasonal variation	Sales budget
Quarter 1	178,000	+ 12,820	190,820
Quarter 2	182,500	+ 14,805	197,305
Quarter 3	187,000	−5,070	181,930
Quarter 4	191,500	−22,555	168,945

(d) £39,000

The overhead cost is represented by

$y = £10,000 + £0.25x$ where x = number of orders

Orders are estimated as follows, using the given formula which combines regression analysis and a time series model.

$$\text{Number of orders} = (100,000 + (240 \times 30)) \times \text{Index value}$$
$$= (100,000 + 7,200) \times 1.08$$
$$= 115,776$$

Using $y = £10,000 + £0.25x$ where x = number of orders = 115,776

The overhead cost is therefore= $£10,000 + (£0.25 \times 115,776) = £38,944$

= £39,000 to the nearest £1,000.

Task 3

	October £	November £	December £
Purchases	120,000	130,000	140,000
Total sales	**192,000**	**208,000**	**224,000**
Split:			
Cash sales (30%)	57,600	62,400	67,200
Credit sales (70%)	134,400	145,600	156,800

	Working	Oct cash received £	Nov cash received £	Dec cash received £	y/e trade receivables £
Cash sales		57,600	62,400	67,200	
Cash from Credit sales:					
October	134,400 × 80%	0	107,520	0	0
October	134,400 × 20%	0	0	26,880	0
November	145,600 × 80%		0	116,480	0
November	145,600 × 20%		0	0	29,120
December	156,800 × 100%	0	0	0	156,800
Total		57,600	169,920	210,560	185,920

Task 4

Cash budget

	Jan £'000	Feb £'000	March £'000	April £'000
Receipts				
Fee on sale (W1)	54	63	99	144
Receipt on sale of vehicles	—	—	—	20
	54	63	99	164
Payments				
Salaries (9 × £35,000/12)	26.25	26.25	26.25	26.25
Bonus (W2)			6.3	12.6
Variable expenses (W3)	9	13.5	22.5	27
Fixed overheads	4.3	4.3	4.3	4.3
Interest on loan			3.0	
Tax liability	—	—	—	95.80
	39.55	44.05	62.35	165.95
Net cash flow	14.45	18.95	36.65	(1.95)
Balance b/fwd	(40.00)	(25.55)	(6.6)	30.05
Balance c/fwd	(25.55)	(6.6)	30.05	28.10
Working 1				
	Jan	Feb	March	April
Receipts				
Unit sales	10	15	25	30
	£'000	£'000	£'000	£'000
Income (£5,400 × numbers sold)	54	81	135	162
Received				
– 1/3 in month of sale	18	27	45	54
– 2/3 in following month				
(January receipt relates to December sale)	36	36	54	90
	54	63	99	144

Working 2				
	Jan	Feb	March	April
Unit sales	10	15	25	30
	£'000	£'000	£'000	£'000
Bonus based on numbers sold over 20	0	0	5	10
– £140 × 9 × numbers sold over 20	0	0	6.3	12.6
Working 3				
	Jan	Feb	March	April
Income	54	81	135	162
	£'000	£'000	£'000	£'000
Variable overheads at 16.67%				
	9	13.5	22.5	27

Task 5

(a)

	Workings	Period 3 £	Period 4 £	Period 5 £
Period 1 sales	£144,000 × 37%	53,280		
Period 2 sales	£151,500 × 60%	90,900		
Period 2 sales	£151,500 × 37%		56,055	
Period 3 sales	£145,450 × 1.05 × 40%×98%	59,867		
Period 3 sales	£145,450 × 1.05 × 30%		45,817	
Period 3 sales	£145,450 × 1.05 × 30%			45,817
Period 4 sales	£139,000 × 1.05 × 40%×98%		57,212	
Period 4 sales	£139,000 × 1.05 × 30%			43,785
Period 5 sales	£162,300 × 1.05 × 40%×98%			66,803
Total receipts from customers		**204,047**	**159,084**	**156,405**

(b)

	Period 3 £	Period 4 £	Period 5 £
Original receipts from customers	144,180	143,325	137,217
Revised receipts from customers	204,047	159,084	156,405
Overall increase/(decrease) in sales receipts	**+59,867**	**+15,759**	**+19,188**

Cost of prompt payment discount	Workings	Period 3 £	Period 4 £	Period 5 £
Period 3 sales	£145,450 × 1.05 × 40% × 2%	−1,222		
Period 4 sales	£139,000 × 1.05 × 40% × 2%		−1,168	
Period 5 sales	£162,300 × 1.05 × 40% × 2%			−1,363

Task 6

(a)

	Budgeted cash flows £	Actual cash flows £	Variance £
Cash sales	32,500	28,600	−3,900
Receipts from credit customers	234,000	198,760	−35,240
Sale of machinery	0	7,500	+7,500
Payments to credit suppliers	(124,700)	(91,200)	+33,500
Wages and salaries	(35,600)	(30,200)	+5,400
General expenses	(14,600)	(10,300)	+4,300
Capital expenditure	0	(20,000)	−20,000
Drawings	(30,000)	(35,000)	−5,000
Net cash flows	61,600	48,160	−13,440
Opening balance	32,500	32,500	0
Closing balance	94,100	80,660	−13,440

(b)

Some customers, who previously bought goods on credit, are taking advantage of lower prices offered on cash sales	Reduction in receipts from credit sales
A machine needed to be replaced unexpectedly when it broke down	Increased capital expenditure
Material costs have decreased	Reduction in payments to suppliers
Large orders necessitated additional overtime working	Increased payments for wages

Task 7

(a) average inventory holding period + average trade receivables' collection period – average trade payables' payment period

(b) Reduce the time taken to produce its product as this will reduce the inventory holding period

(c) Decreasing the trade receivables' collection period by 2 days

(d) Order size for bulk discounts is 10,000

Number of orders per year = 60,000/10,000 = 6

Annual ordering cost = 6 × £6 = £36

Inventory cost = 60,000 × £12 × 99% = £712,800

Total cost of inventory with discount = 712,800 + 36 = £712,836

Task 8

(a)

Option 1	Month-end balance £	Overdraft cost £
January	3,950	500
February	(6,700)	67
March	(11,200)	112
April	(2,400)	24
May	(10,800)	108
June	1,250	0
Total cost		£811

Option 2	£
Total interest	960
Monthly interest payment (Jan – Dec)	80

(b)

Email

To: fd@company.co.uk   **Date:** Today

From: aatstudent@company.co.uk   **Subject:** Raising finance

The information supplied indicates that the company will have a maximum overdrawn

balance of £ 11,300 during the year.

If the company selects the overdraft option the cost for the year will be £ 811 ,

whereas the annual cost of the short term bank loan is £ 960 .

I recommend that the bank overdraft option be selected as this will have the

lowest cost for the company. As the business is seasonal the bank overdraft

provides the most flexibility . Although the interest rate on the loan is lower ,

interest has to be paid for 12 months, despite the business bank account being

In credit for more than six months of the year.

Task 9

To: Financial Controller
From: Adviser
Subject: Working capital
Date: 27 September 20X2

This report covers the benefits of factoring

Benefits of factoring

(1) The business can pay its suppliers promptly, and so be able to take advantage of any early payment discounts that are available.

(2) Optimum inventory levels can be maintained, because the business will have enough cash to pay for the inventories it needs.

(3) Growth can be financed through sales rather than by injecting fresh external capital.

(4) The business gets finance linked to its volume of sales. In contrast, overdraft limits tend to be determined by historical balance sheets.

(5) The managers of the business do not have to spend their time on the problems of slow paying receivables and with non-recourse factoring the risk of irrecoverable debts lies with the factor.

(6) The business does not incur the costs of running its own sales ledger department, and can use the expertise of receivable management that the factor has.

(7) Because they are managing a number of sales ledgers, factors can manage receivables more efficiently than individual businesses through economies of scale.

Existing receivables collection costs

	£
Irrecoverable debts (3% × 90% × £2.5m)	67,500
Salary of sales ledger administrator	12,500
Cost of financing debts (90% × (2.5/12) × 12% × £2.5m)	56,250
Total cost	136,250

Receivables collection costs under factor

	£
Irrecoverable debts (borne by factor)	Nil
Cost of advancing funds (90% × 80% × (1/12) × 15% × £2.5m	22,500
Cost of financing remaining debts (90% × 20% × (1/12) × 12% × £2.5m)	4,500
Charge for factoring services (4% × 90% × £2.5m)	90,000
One-off payment to factor	12,000
Total cost	129,000

Hence it is worthwhile to factor the debts.

Task 10

Factors to consider when investing any cash surplus

The cash budget for Property Co shows an increase in sales over the period, which suggests higher sales as the spring approaches. However, the payment of tax in April means that a trend of increasing net cash flows is temporarily reversed.

The company needs to consider the following when investing any surpluses:

(i) Short-term investments with no capital risk would be suitable as these may be called upon at any time. Short-term investments include bank deposit accounts, certificates of deposit, term bills and gilts, which are short-dated. In choosing between these, the company will need to consider the size of the surplus, the length of time it is available, the yield offered and the risk associated with each instrument.

(ii) On an annual basis, look at any surpluses and invest these in longer-term higher yield assets. The company will most probably call on these at some stage to fund expansion but needs to pick the investments carefully.

The investment of cash balances is part of the treasury function of a company. It is unlikely that Property Co is of a size to sustain a full time treasury activity but nonetheless there is a definite benefit in closely managing any surpluses.

Notes

Notes

292

Notes

Notes